Essential

New York

by

DAVID WICKERS AND CHARLOTTE ATKINS

David Wickers is the travel correspondent of
The Sunday Times and Travel Editor of
Marie Claire.
Charlotte Atkins is Travel Editor of *Woman's Own*
and a regular contributor to
The Sunday Times.

Produced by AA Publishing

**Written by David Wickers and
Charlotte Atkins
Peace and Quiet section
by Paul Sterry
Original photoghraphy
by Douglas Corrance**

First published January 1991
Revised second edition May 1994
Reprinted March 1995

Edited, designed and produced by
AA Publishing.
© The Automobile Association 1994.
Maps © The Automobile Association
1994.

Distributed in the United Kingdom
by AA Publishing, Norfolk House,
Priestley Road, Basingstoke,
Hampshire, RG24 9NY.

A CIP catalogue record for this book
is available from the British Library.

ISBN 0 7495 0872 8

The contents of this publication are
believed correct at the time of
printing. Nevertheless, the
publishers cannot be held
responsible for any errors or
omissions or for changes in the
details given in this guide or for the
consequences of any reliance on the
information provided by the same.
Assessments of attractions, hotels,
restaurants and so forth are based
upon the author's own experience
and, therefore, descriptions given in
this guide necessarily contain an
element of subjective opinion which
may not reflect the publisher's
opinion or dictate a reader's own
experience on another occasion.
**We have tried to ensure accuracy
in this guide, but things do change
and we would be grateful if
readers would advise us of any
inaccuracies they may encounter**.

Published by AA Publishing, a
trading name of Automobile
Association Developments Limited,
whose registered office is Norfolk
House, Priestley Road, Basingstoke,
Hampshire, RG24 9NY.
Registered number 1878835.

Colour separation: Mullis Morgan
Ltd., London

Printed by: Printers Trento, S.R.L.,
Italy

Front cover picture: Statue of Liberty

CONTENTS

This book employs a simple
rating system to help choose
which places to visit:

✓	'top ten'

◆◆◆   do not miss
◆◆   see if you can
◆   worth seeing if you
      have time

INTRODUCTION

New York, New York! A bird's eye view of the Big Apple

INTRODUCTION

New York is uncompromisingly urban. It is noisy, dirty, crime-ridden, aggressive and overwhelmingly energetic. There is no other city in the world quite like it. You might end up loving it or loathing it, but it's impossible to feel indifference towards it.

There is one person whose love for his hometown should qualify him for a space on the New York Convention and Visitor Bureau payroll. What Woody Allen hasn't portrayed about his favourite city on cinema screens around the world probably isn't worth knowing. Apart from *Manhattan*, *Annie Hall*, and *Hannah and Her Sisters*, the city has proved a worthy backdrop for many more successful films, not to mention endless TV 'cop' series. No wonder New York feels familiar the minute you set foot in it. New York is a network of neighbourhoods, each with its distinctive ambience that can make the mere crossing of a street a few small steps for the tourist but a series of giant strides in terms of cultural transition.

Ever since New York became the principal port of immigration for the world's huddled masses, various ethnic groups settled and re-established traditional ways and means in specific areas. Chinatown hums of old Hangchow, for example, while the atmosphere in Little Italy, on the other side of Canal Street's discount stores, is almost Neapolitan, as different from the next door Orientals as chalk from dolcelatte. During the Chinese New Year celebrations in February or the September Festa di San Gennaro, the respective national flavours are so exclusive that you will be convinced that the *New York Times* are all airmail editions specially flown in for the American tourists.

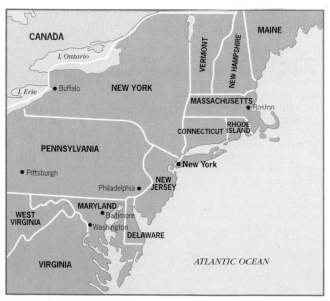

BACKGROUND

There was a time when only the British and the Dutch had landed on these shores. The river which runs down the western flank of the borough of Manhattan brought Henry Hudson to this virgin territory in 1609. He was an English explorer, sailing the good ship *Half Moon* on behalf of the Dutch East India Company, and he gave his name to the river. But Hudson had, in fact, already been pipped at the post in 1524 by Italian Giovanni da Verrazano, who happened upon New York Bay while searching for a northwest passage. They named a bridge after him.

The settlement was tossed like a ball between the Dutch and the British for the next few years, first coming into the hands of the Dutch, as Nieuw Amsterdam, in 1623. In 1664 Governor Peter Stuyvesant surrendered the city to the British, who were led by the Duke of York, and the name was changed to New York. The Dutch wrenched it back in 1673, this time preferring the title New Orange. The following year the British were back in power.

Independence Day in 1783 marked the end of the American War of Independence against the British colonial power, and another turning point in New York's history. Washington was sworn in as first President at Federal Hall in New York, the first capital of the Federal Government in 1789. The city of New York was now the official capital of the nation and the state.

Almost a hundred years later the five boroughs, Manhattan, Brooklyn, the Bronx, Queens and Staten Island, were formed. As a group they comprised Greater New York, at the time the largest city in the world with a population of over three million.

Manhattan, the central borough and the hub of New York's cultural and financial life, is the area which most visitors see. Because of the sheer density of people stacked on top of each other, today's Manhattan has become a showcase of extremes of wealth and poverty, opportunity and deprivation. The gamut of social inequalities, normally found spread over much greater distances, or else disguised in the patchwork of less orderly planned urban areas, can be experienced during an afternoon stroll in Manhattan along a single avenue. To see both sides of New York, pick one of the fashionable East Side avenues – Madison perhaps; start in the mid-50s and head north, passing the galleries, boutiques, epicurean stores and apartments of the rich, and continue north until you reach the borders of hardcore Harlem (though if you are white do not expect to feel too welcome), where nearly half the residents live on welfare.

Even if you find figures meaningless, New York's vital statistics are mind-boggling –

Queens, New York's largest, borough, was once the home of America's film industry

3,500 churches and synagogues, 200 skyscrapers, 150 museums, 500 galleries, 238 theatres, 100 night-clubs, 50 dance spots and 90,000 homeless. If you do not suffer from acute vertigo opt for an early, bird's-eye view of Manhattan so that its elongated, insular format and the grid of concrete canyons fall into perspective. The Empire State Building is still the favourite viewing point, although it is now dwarfed by the twin towers of the World Trade Center, where you can sip *pina coladas* in the cocktail lounge, called the Windows of the World, while studying Manhattan's night-time glitter, both the outside view and the inside glamour.
In one respect, the clichés of New York never seem to change. The tall buildings, crowded sidewalks, gridlocks at traffic intersections and the day and night wail of sirens soon come to feel like second nature. There really are stretched limos, gliding silently past Tiffany's and other grand stores, the dowagers inside cushioned from the street incredibilities. And the wisps of steam do rise magically from manholes, especially on cold winter days.
But look closer, peel away the veneer and you will find a constant state of flux which leaves even the natives reeling. Restaurants open and close, shops relocate and new monster buildings change the symmetry of the skyline. Enjoy a meal in an Italian restaurant on Broadway and, when you return six months later, it will be Mexican. The *Zagat New York City Restaurant Survey,* an essential guide to the city's best eateries, even includes a section called *Noteworthy Closings.*

THE CITY LAYOUT

Manhattan

Although New York consists of five boroughs – Manhattan, Queens, the Bronx, Brooklyn and Staten Island – most of the things you will want to see and do are in Manhattan. This elongated island is bordered to the east by the East River, to the west by the Hudson and partitioned from the Bronx by the Harlem River at the north end. Manhattan's streets and avenues are mostly laid out in a grid and, as every fan of American musicals will recall, 'the Bronx is up and the Battery's down'.

With its streets laid at right-angles, avenues running north to south, streets east to west, the city map looks like a chessboard. Streets are numbered from south to north and according to whether they lie east or west of Fifth Avenue; if an address is 130 East 45th Street, for example, you know it lies on the east side of town. Avenues begin at First on the East River and work their way west to 12th on the Hudson River. Among the anomalies to remember are that Lexington, Park and Madison Avenues all run between Third and Fifth Avenues, and that the officially named Avenue of the Americas is always known as Sixth. The most famous of all is Broadway, which slices diagonally across the island from 'downtown' southeast to 'uptown' northwest; that is, from Wall Street to the Bronx. In the Upper East Side there is also York Avenue, which runs between First Avenue and the East River/Franklin D Roosevelt

The confusion of the skyline belies the street layout's logic

Drive. And in the Lower East Side of town, Avenues A, B, C and D fall between First Avenue and the East River Drive in an area which is known to the locals at Alphabet City.

If you explore Manhattan by numbers you will not get lost, except perhaps at the southern end where the rules of symmetry run amok, and the streets have names, not numbers, and often lie at funny angles. Look up from your map if you feel disorientated: if you can see the Empire State Building you're looking north; if the towers of the World Trade Center are before you, you're probably facing south.

Downtown

Downtown Manhattan, commonly agreed to be everything south of 23rd Street, is New York at its most non-conformist. By day it's the place for avant garde shops and art galleries; by night for restaurants, bars and nightclubs. 'Downtown' roughly encompasses Greenwich Village, the East and West Villages, SoHo, TriBeCa, Chinatown, Little Italy, the Lower East Side, Chelsea, Battery Park and the Financial District, usually referred to by the name of its most famous artery, Wall Street. Here, after blocks of radical and ethnic lifestyles, jacket and tie conventionalism re-establishes itself with a jolt.

Greenwich Village ✓

Greenwich Village has, over recent years, grown in respectability as real estate prices have forced its more bohemian residents first into the West Village and, more recently, the East Village, bordered by the Bowery with its detritus of heavy drinkers. Greenwich's Washington Square, however, home of New York University, still symbolises the hub of alternative living, casting a magnetic spell over aspiring Bob Dylans and Joan Baezes and enticing them from home towns across middle America to trail their feet in the fountain and be 'where it's at'. Or was. Moving directly westward, the area becomes predominantly gay, particularly along Christopher Street (with its Kiss My Cookies candy store) as far as the river and the now fast disappearing 'heavy leather' hangouts (the Anvil, Ramrod, etc). Also gone is the old, cast-iron West Side elevated highway, torn down by the city as its structure rusted and weakened with the passing years.

Part of the Village area's attraction lies in its lack of high-rise buildings. Its bars, pubs, clubs, cafés and coffee houses still inspire a lingering, discursive clientele, despite the looming presence of high finance and yuppiedom just around the block. A cappuccino at Café Figaro on the corner of Bleecker and MacDougal Streets, famous hangout of the '50s Beat writers, or an iced tea at Café Borgia on the opposite corner, is now the closest New York comes to a Latin Quarter: a throwback to the days of Lucy Mabel Dodge, one of the Village's first eccentrics, who

CITY LAYOUT

entertained the wealthy, radical
literati at her Greenwich Village
home.

Lower East Side
The Lower East Side is New
York's old Jewish section,
traditionally a haven for those
escaping religious persecution
throughout the 19th century. As
many of the Jews prospered
and moved into mainstream
Manhattan, their place was
taken by more recent
immigrant groups, including
blacks and Puerto Ricans. Most
of the Lower East Side is an
unattractive sprawl of high-rise
apartments.
For the visitor, the most
colourful event is the Sunday

morning Orchard Street market
(bargain clothes, furniture and
bric-à-brac), traditionally
followed by a pastrami on rye
sandwich at Katz's Deli on East
Houston.

SoHo
Once the city's ugly duckling,
SoHo is now one of the
wealthiest patches of real estate
in the world. Originally known
as Hell's Hundred Acres, this
26-block district South of
Houston Street (pronounced
Howston), hence SoHo, was a
satanic nightmare of
sweatshops and warehouses.
First squatted by artists, SoHo
has flourished since the '60s
into a creative ghetto of around

a hundred galleries that look like restaurants that look like bars that look like stores that look like galleries. Most are focused on West Broadway and stay open from Tuesday to Saturday, from around 10.00-18.00 hrs. Some also open on Sundays.

To the 1990s New Yorker, SoHo means unattainable real estate. The high rents have forced the original artists out to neighbouring TriBeCa, NoHo and even over the bridge to Brooklyn. Nowadays a 'loft' in one of the converted cast-iron buildings with a front laddered by its fire escape is a sure sign of having made it in the artistic jungle.

A child of the 'Sixties, SoHo, New York's artists' colony, is quick to catch the eye

Contemporary man, according to Woody Allen, is alienated. 'He has seen the ravages of war, he has known natural catastrophes, he has been to the singles bars.' Although most are to be found on the Upper East Side (Friday's, Adam's Apple, etc), SoHo's Broome Street Bar (corner of Broome and West Broadway) is the West Side equivalent. If you don't meet you can eat – hamburgers, sandwiches and other fancy pub grub.

There are two occasions on which to visit SoHo. During the week, most of the people milling around the streets will be local residents going about the daily business of buying their groceries or replenishing their tubes of oils and guache. And on Saturdays the crowds arrive in from the suburbs of

CITY LAYOUT

New Jersey to window-shop or just rub shoulders with the creative forces that make SoHo one of the world's most dynamic urban pockets.

Little Italy

On the other side of Broadway, an unofficial border, lies Little Italy, which draws New Yorkers primarily to eat in its restaurants and coffee bars and shop in its bakeries and delis. A cappuccino from a hissing Gaggia and a mouthwatering *dolce* at a table at Ferrara's on Grand Street, for example, is as authentic a taste of Italy as anything you will find in the old country. But the biggest threat to the future of Little Italy is the slow encroachment of Chinatown, on the south side of Canal Street.

Chinatown

Canal Street is tacky at any time, but almost unbearable in the heat of mid-summer. The strip's historic origins are self-evident: a 40-foot (12m) wide canal ran along here at the beginning of the 19th century to drain the waters of New York's reservoir, Collect Pond, into the Hudson River. Today the water has been replaced with a steady flow of people, and the street is one long, noisy strip of electrical shops, discount clothing stores, fluorescent handwritten 'sale' signs and the backs of numerous sales staff sitting on raised seats like tennis umpires, watching out for in-store theft.

On the southern side of Canal Street lies Chinatown, home to half of New York's 150,000 Chinese, the largest overseas community of Chinese in the world. The district is so completely self-sufficient, it's almost as though the entire community has been plucked from the Far East and laid to rest in Manhattan, its inhabitants unaware of the transition. It has its own theatres, eight daily newspapers, shops, restaurants, street signs, even miniature pagodas on top of its public phone boxes.

Make for the intersection of Mott and Pell Streets for the heart of Chinatown. This is where the Chinese New Year revellers focus their parades. Take a look at May May Coffee Shop, Wing Fat Company Produce, Sam Wo Restaurant and Lung Fung Chinese Bakery. Even Baskin Robbins is decorated with red and gold pagodas. Shops like Kam Man are mega-bazaars of fish, meat, exotic vegetables, fruits and Oriental cooking utensils. A stroll along Bowery, Pell, Bayard and Boyers streets and you have absorbed the spirit of the Far East as much as of New York.

To the rest of New York, Chinatown is one huge dining table – and it doesn't matter where you sit or what you eat, the bill always seems to be the same: inexpensive. But a word of warning to the more fickle feasters: Chinatown menus embrace a wide range of ingredients that may offend the more squeamish palates.

TriBeCa

Roughly defined by Canal Street, Broadway and West Street, TriBeCa is an acronym for the Triangle Below Canal

Street. As SoHo rents have risen to prohibitive levels, several alternative creative enclaves have sprung up. TriBeCa was one of the first to absorb the shift in artistic talent, its former spice warehouses rapidly gentrified into living space for the new inhabitants. In recent months several excellent small

Once an area of spice warehouses, TriBeCa has been spiced up with galleries and restaurants

CITY LAYOUT

restaurants have opened with more a European/chef-inspired flavour than the majority of New York eating houses. But the art deco Odeon Café is still the trendiest restaurant and bar in the district – Robert de Niro, Woody Allen and Warren Beatty are frequently noted there by the gossip columnists. Interesting spots include Duane Park at the end of Duane Street, a small, natural oasis still ringed with cheese, butter and egg wholesalers and benches for viewing the Downtown skyline. But the main sight is undoubtedly the view from the Clocktower on top of the former New York Life Insurance Company, now the Clocktower Gallery of the Institute for Art and Urban Resources. Other attractions are the Artist's Space Gallery, a second-floor rabbit-warren of local exhibits at 105 Hudson Street at Franklin Street; and lunch at the cast-iron Thomas Street Inn.

Financial District

This is a ruthless bunch of oversized Lego pieces, squeezed onto the island's southern tip, a sight best appreciated from the Staten Island Ferry – twice in fact, by day and by night, to get the full effect. If Manhattan were to be floated, the sheer weight of buildings carried on the southern tip, competing with the low rise north, would tip it like a see-saw, pivoting somewhere around the Canal Street area.

Between eight and nine in the morning the streets of the Financial District are frenzied, with thousands of businessmen ticking away on White Rabbit schedules. At five, they are back on the streets, disappearing into waiting limos or underground to the subway. At night Wall Street and the surrounding canyons are transformed into a commercial desert.

For the visitor there are a few essential viewings, including the one from the Observation Deck of the World Trade Center (or the restaurant if you can afford the prices). Even the most cynical tourist will feel a hint of magic on first seeing the Wall Street sign, but the New York Stock Exchange (gallery open to visitors) is only of mild interest. From Battery Park you can see the Statue of Liberty, and also catch a tour boat for closer inspection, as well as the boat to Ellis Island and the ferry to Staten Island. But the most interesting area for the visitor is the restored South Street Seaport and its Museum of Historic Ships (see page 41).

Midtown

The average visitor spends more time in midtown Manhattan than anywhere else in town, not only because his hotel is probably in the area, but also because so are most of New York's famous stores – Fifth Avenue slices through the heart of midtown – as well as a good deal of the entertainment, with the theatres of Broadway and Times Square falling within its boundaries.

Working your way north from downtown, you come first to Murray Hill on the East Side, a predominantly residential area and of little interest. To the west is the Garment District, again of marginal interest to out-of-towners, who are forced to spend most of their time trying to avoid the display rails of polythened dresses being speedily wheeled along the streets and sidewalks with utter disregard for the welfare of pedestrians. Three-quarters of all the women's and children's clothes in the US originate from these few blocks.

Temples of commerce crowd Manhattan's Financial District

On the southern fringes of the Garment District are Tin Pan Alley, or West 28th Street, where music publishers used to peddle songs to artists and producers from the nearby theatres, and the Flower Market in Chelsea, where pot plants and cut flowers are stored before being launched onto the wholesale market. Madison Square Garden is also here, venue for both sporting and mega rock events, and Pennsylvania railroad station. Grand Central Terminal is the bigger and better known railway landmark of midtown Manhattan, well worth going to see, even if you don't have a train to catch. Its main entrance

is on 42nd Street, the city's most famous crosstown thoroughfare, although today it is mostly made up of sleazy cinemas. Times Square (currently undergoing restoration) is the unofficial heart of New York and again, although attracting a good deal of low life at night, is filled with milling theatregoers on their way to or from Broadway.

Uptown Central

The most distinctive landmark of uptown Manhattan is Central Park, which runs right up the middle, from 59th Street all the way to 110th Street, dividing the two distinct upper halves of the city. (See page 38).

Upper West Side

Manhattan is a place of shifting frontiers, of areas whose style or function become re-defined by necessity or fashion. The best and most recent example is the metamorphosis of Upper West Side's Columbus Avenue, one of the area's three main arteries (Broadway and Amsterdam are the other two) from a rather seedy west side through-route to a 'hot' area, with all the right boutiques, restaurants, fancy and wholefood stores and Parisian-type sidewalk cafés where, screened from cold winds, couples sit perched at marble-topped bars, sharing a *café au lait* or two.

Bordered by Riverside Drive to the west and Central Park to the east, and spliced in two by Broadway, the Upper West Side's stores, bars, restaurants and other places for offloading money are blossoming. Even the classier East Siders now venture across the great Fifth Avenue divide, particularly at the weekends.

The Upper West Side was not always so smart. The Lincoln Center, for example, focal point for the performing arts, sits where some of the city's worst slums once stood, a core of tenements made famous as the backdrop for *West Side Story*.

Lincoln Center arts complex is the stage for the world's performers

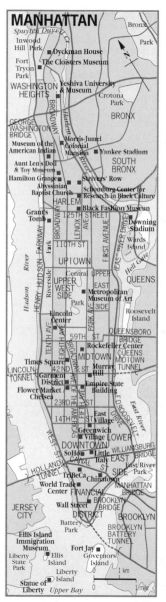

Dazzling neon in Times Square, for many the centre of Manhattan

They were razed to the ground in the '60s and replaced with a complex whose main aim was to raise the tone of the area. Since then the gentrification of the Upper West Side has moved slowly north, a block at a time, and now stops more or less at the north end of Central Park.

Upper East Side

New York's historic roots don't dry up once you step beyond Chinatown, Little Italy and the Lower East Side. On the wealthier Upper East Side, between Central Park and the East River, roughly between 77th and 96th Streets, you will find Yorkville, a country village in the 18th century and now a largely German neighbourhood, complete with beer halls, delicatessens such as Schaller and Weber (1654 2nd Avenue) and *bratwurst* shops. Today a million New Yorkers claim German ancestry, given away in names of restaurants like Café Geiger and Kleine Konditorei. There's also a Middle Eastern 'belly belt' in the Upper East Side and a mini-Czechoslovakia. Most of

CITY LAYOUT

the up-market apartment houses are also located on this side of the Park, the most exclusive being on Fifth Avenue with windows or, even more impressive, balconies, terraces and even roof gardens overlooking the greenery. Most of New York's museums are located in the Upper East Side, including the Met (Metropolitan Museum of Art), Whitney, Guggenheim, Cooper-Hewitt and Frick. It is also home to Bloomingdale's department store, known locally as Bloomies, and Gracie Mansion, the mayor's official residence facing the East River.

Harlem and the North

Harlem, the poorest ghetto among Manhattan's many districts and almost entirely inhabited by Puerto Ricans and blacks, lies far uptown with 125th Street and Lenox Avenue the real hub. First known as Nieuw Haarlem by the Dutch, the area was established in 1658 by Peter Stuyvesant. For almost 200 years it was little more than rural farmland, but became a rapidly growing suburb when the Harlem Railroad was built in the 1830s. In 1910 the construction of the subway caused many blacks from lower Manhattan to move into Harlem. During World War I there was a further influx from the Deep South of the US and the West Indies (which stimulated the 'Harlem Renaissance' of the 1920s), more recently followed by Puerto Ricans and others from South America. Today, Harlem is cautiously making its way back on to the visitor's

sightseeing agenda. Several companies now offer tours that take in both slums and sights, churches and museums, Spanish as well as Black Harlem. Most include the restored Morris-Jumel Colonial Mansion, which served as Washington's headquarters during the American Revolution, the enormous food market in Spanish Harlem, the Apollo Theatre, where James Brown and other leading black entertainers have performed, the Strivers' Row houses of the upwardly mobile, Hamilton Grange (home of founding father Alexander Hamilton), the Schomburg Center for Research in Black Culture and the Abyssinian Baptist Church, the largest of its kind in the world. There are also theme tours covering Harlem Gospel music (Sundays only), Soul Food and evening Champagne Jazz Safaris. Companies include New York Big Apple Tours, 203 East 94th Street (tel: 410 4190); Harlem Spirituals, 1457 Broadway (tel: 302 2595); Harlem Your Way! Tours Unlimited, 129 West 130th Street (tel: 690 1687) and Harlem Renaissance Tours, 18 East 105th Street (tel: 722 9534).

Brooklyn

Brooklyn, together with Queens, forms the western tip of Long Island, a 125-mile (200km)-long peninsula that runs parallel to the mainland, separated by Long Island Sound, a playground for yachtsmen. By far the biggest of New York's five boroughs in terms of inhabitants, Brooklyn's 2.3 million population is almost double that of Manhattan. In fact, Brooklyn was a separate conglomerate of villages and towns until it was annexed by its big sister in 1898, much to the chagrin of many locals. But memories are short and now the people who live in Brooklyn Heights, the most fashionable part, will tell you that their district is a slice of Manhattan that drifted away across the East River. Facing South Street

Almost New England, Brooklyn Heights is east of Manhattan

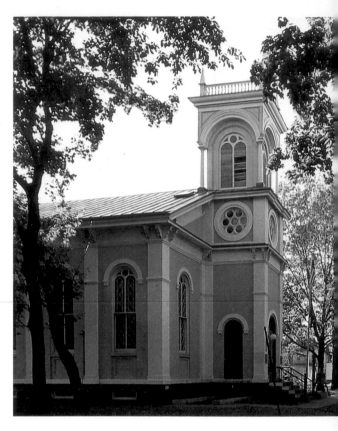

Seaport, the Heights is Brooklyn at her wealthiest: a broken line of pre-war apartment blocks with names like Willow, Pineapple and Cranberry. Orange Street, with its wooden-framed New England style houses, winds up at a promenade that overlooks the harbour; while Montague Street is the place for coffee in a café. Many of the rich and famous who were either born or flourished in Brooklyn have their names engraved on the Celebrity Path in the district's most famous attraction, the Brooklyn Botanic Garden. Tiptoe past Danny Kaye and tread softly on George Gershwin, Woody Allen, Mae West and Mary Tyler Moore.

Staten Island
According to Henry David Thoreau, the whole of Staten Island 'is like a garden and affords fine scenery'. Five miles

A short ferry ride across New York Harbor, Snug Harbor nestles on Staten Island's north coast

Verrazano-Narrows Bridge, linking Staten Island to Brooklyn.

Today the appeal of the island is limited. To most visitors its only draw is the return ferry ride (the only means of public transportation to the island), which at 50 cents is still an unbelievable bargain, and which offers unbeatable views of the lower Manhattan skyline. It operates around the clock, every half hour.

There are also a few attractions that make it worth stepping ashore, if only for a couple of hours' breathing space from the steamy metropolis: the Snug Harbor Cultural Center, for example, and the Staten Island Zoo in Barrett Park which deserves a visit for its excellent reptile collection.

The 1675 Conference House marks the spot where Benjamin Franklin, John Adams and Edward Rutledge met with British Admiral Lord Howe during the War of Independence, in an unsuccessful effort to make peace in September 1776. And Richmondtown is a quaint, and just a little too cute, restored 17th-century American village, complete with craftspeople dressed in historic costumes. On a more hardy level, visitors can hike through High Rock Park, or ride a horse through Clay Pit Pond Park, a bucolic mixture of swamps, bogs, ponds, woodland and streams.

(8km) and a 20-minute ferry ride from southern Manhattan, the island is probably the closest New York comes to the country. It was first discovered by Giovanni da Verrazano in 1524 and its transformation from rural back-of-beyond to a desirable place to live came with the construction of the

The Bronx
New York's only mainland borough was 350 years old in

CITY LAYOUT

1989, marking the time in 1639 when Johannes Bronck, a Danish immigrant, bought the 500 acres (200 hectares) from the Dutch West India Company. Together with his nine brothers he owned a large chunk of what is now New York State. As recently as World War II, they were still farming in the Bronx; in the mid-19th century the area was largely wilderness, and Edgar Allen Poe brought his wife to live here in the hope that the clean, country air would cure her tuberculosis (their cottage can be visited).

Modern day Bronx, alas, has changed dramatically: its 42 square miles (108 sq km) now has almost two million citizens. If the Bronx was ever beginning to woo cautious tourists, Tom Wolfe's best-selling novel *The Bonfire of the Vanities* will have undone all the hard work. Contrary to popular belief it's only the South Bronx, with its Hispanic/black poverty, which is a definite no-go area for the visitor. North of 100th Street, you will see a whole different side, almost a taste of what New York was like before real estate and drug dealers set to work on its neighbourhoods. In Tremont, for example, along Arthur Avenue and its neighbouring streets around Our Lady of Mount Carmel Roman Catholic Church, a Southern Italian heritage is evident in neighbourhood stores, bakeries and delicatessens selling home-made spaghetti, ravioli and mozzarella. There are even a few pushcarts left, trading in spite of the shops.

The Bronx is well worth a visit for sights like the 1748 Van Cortlandt Mansion, Wave Hill (former home of Theodore Roosevelt, Mark Twain and Arturo Toscanini) and the 1758 Valentine-Varian House. The Bronx is also home to the biggest and best zoo in the city, New York Botanical Garden; and the Yankees are still pulling the baseball fans in Yankee Stadium.

Queens

Most visitors spend their first and last New York moments in Queens, New York's largest borough, watching their watches in JF Kennedy Airport. Rarely do they spend any time there in between flights, which is a shame but quite understandable, since most of the borough's attractions are watered-down versions of those across the water. The main exception is Astoria, home to the largest concentration of Greeks outside Greece. There are, of course, lots of good Greek restaurants in the area. Until the rise of Hollywood in the '30s, Astoria was *the* centre for American film-making (it is still the fourth largest in the US) and the American Museum of the Moving Image is one of the city's newest and most popular museums. Other sights include the 1661 Bowne House, a shrine of religious freedom and King Manor, once the estate of Rufus King, a signatory of the US Constitution.

Brooklyn Bridge, over a century old, spans East River

WHAT TO SEE

Churches, Monuments and Statues

◆◆◆
BROOKLYN BRIDGE

The two greatest works of architecture in New York, according to Paul Goldberger, author of *The City Observed,* are not even buildings. One is Central Park (see page 38); the other is Brooklyn Bridge, whose fine, lacy framework played a romantic role in Woody Allen's *Manhattan.* For 20 years, from 1883–1903, the bridge was the largest suspension bridge in the world and its two towers, though it's hard to believe today, were considered gigantic. In 1983 New York, along with the rest of the nation, celebrated the bridge's centenary. The most intimate way to appreciate both its technology and aesthetics is to walk across (there is a proper footway). If your purse strings can take the strain, have your own celebration in the floating River Café below the bridge on the Brooklyn side.
Subway: Fulton/William Street or, for the restaurant, High Street/Brooklyn Bridge.

◆◆
CATHEDRAL CHURCH OF ST JOHN THE DIVINE
Amsterdam Avenue at West 112th Street
One of the things worth seeing north of the Upper West Side

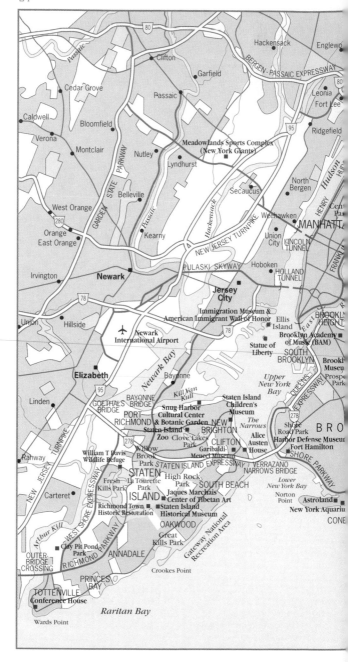

Hackensack

Englewo

Clifton

BERGEN-PASSAIC EXPRESSWAY

Garfield

Leonia

Fort Lee

Cedar Grove

Passaic

Ridgefield

Caldwell

Bloomfield

Verona

GARDEN STATE PARKWAY

Montclair

Nutley

Meadowlands Sports Complex
(New York Giants)

North
Bergen

Hudson

Lyndhurst

Belleville

Secaucus

Weehawken

Cen
Pa

West Orange

Kearny

Union
City

MANHATT

Orange
East Orange

NEW JERSEY TURNPIKE

LINCOLN
TUNNEL

PULASKI SKYWAY

Hoboken

HOLLAND
TUNNEL

Irvington

Newark

Jersey
City

BROOKL
HEIGHT

Union

Hillside

Immigration Museum &
American Immigrant Wall of Honor

Ellis
Island

East

Newark
International Airport

Statue of
Liberty

Brooklyn Academy
of Music (BAM)

SOUTH
BROOKLYN

Brookl
Museu

Elizabeth

Bayonne

Newark Bay

Upper
New York
Bay

QUEENS

Prosp
Park

Linden

BAYONNE
BRIDGE

Kill Van Kull

Staten Island
Children's
Museum

278

Shore
Road Park

BR0

GOETHALS
BRIDGE

PORT
RICHMOND

Snug Harbor
Cultural Center
& Botanic Garden

The
Narrows

Harbor Defense Museu
Fort Hamilton

Staten Island
Zoo

NEW
BRIGHTON

Alice
Austen
House

SHORE PARKWAY

Rahway

William T Davis
Wildlife Refuge

Willow
Brook

Clove Lakes
Park

CLIFTON

Garibaldi

VERRAZANO
NARROWS BRIDGE

Carteret

Fresh
Kills Park

La Tourette
Park

Meucci Museum

STATEN ISLAND EXPRESSWAY

STATEN
ISLAND

High Rock
Park

SOUTH BEACH

Lower
New York Bay

Norton
Point

Clay Pit Pond
Park

Jaques Marchais
Center of Tibetan Art

Astroland

Richmond Town
Historic Restoration

Staten Island
Historical Museum

New York Aquariu

OUTER-
BRIDGE
CROSSING

RICHMOND PARKWAY

OAKWOOD

Great
Kills Park

Gateway National
Recreation Area

CONE

ANNADALE

PRINCES
BAY

Crookes Point

TOTTENVILLE
Conference House

Raritan Bay

Wards Point

Passaic

Hackensack

Passaic

Arthur Kill

WEST SHORE EXPRESSWAY

NEW JERSEY TURNPIKE

HENRY HUD

FRANKL

BROO

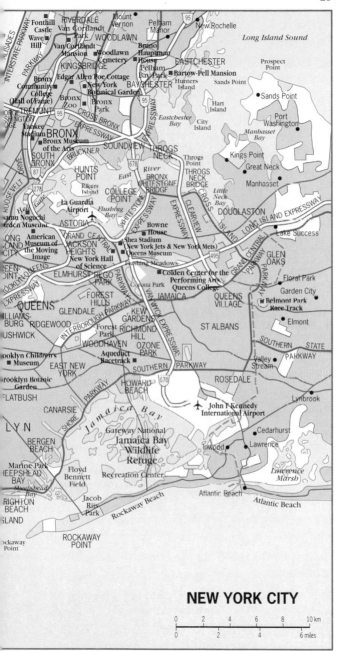

NEW YORK CITY

| 0 | | 2 | | 4 | | 6 | | 8 | | 10 km |

| 0 | | 2 | | 4 | | 6 miles |

WHAT TO SEE

boundary with Harlem. When finished (there is another third still planned) it is expected to be the largest Gothic cathedral in the world and will be capable of holding two full size American football pitches. Outside are 13 acres (5 hectares) of grounds, containing a biblical garden, a Museum of Religious Art, a gymnasium, a shelter for the homeless and a gift shop, as well as art exhibitions and free concerts (tel: 316 7540/7490).
Open: for tours Tuesday to Saturday 11.00hrs, Sunday 12.45hrs.
Subway: 110th Street/Cathedral Parkway.

◆
FEDERAL HALL NATIONAL MEMORIAL
26 Wall Street at Nassau
A Doric temple-style building, marking the spot where George Washington became the nation's first president on April 30, 1789 and where the first congress met the month before. A good place to study America's history through various exhibits, films and 18th century folk music (tel: 264 8711).
Open: Monday to Friday 09.00–17.00hrs. Free.
Subway: Broad Street/Wall Street.

◆
NEW YORK STOCK EXCHANGE
20 Broad Street
Bonfire of the Vanities fans will be itching to see two areas of New York: Park Avenue, fictitious home of Sherman McCoy, and Wall Street, where

The Lion made his billions trading in stocks and shares. The narrowness of Wall Street and the height of the buildings on either side accentuate their intimidation. The focal point of this quite unprepossessing street is the Neo-Classical New York Stock Exchange, the money capital of the world. Look up for the balconies from which ruined traders are said to have jumped to their death rather than face the vast debts incurred by Black Tuesday's share crash on 24 October 1929. The more recent Black Monday had less dramatic consequences. The visitors' gallery has free self-guided tours during trading hours.
Open: Monday to Friday 09.15–16.00hrs. Free tickets at 9am for self-guided tours.
Last tour 15.30hrs.
Subway: Broad Street/Wall Street/Rector Street.

◆◆◆
ST PATRICK'S CATHEDRAL
Fifth Avenue at 50th Street
Seat of the Roman Catholic Archdiocese of New York. Designed by James Renwick and built between 1858 and 1874. The gothic style and plain white interior give it a clinical, sterile atmosphere. It's more impressive from the outside, though dwarfed by its high-rise neighbours (tel: 753 2261).
Open: daily 07.00–20.00hrs.
Subway: 50th/51st/Fifth Avenue

◆
ST PAUL'S CHAPEL
Broadway at Fulton and Vesey Streets
A pretty Georgian structure, beautifully pink and blue

inside. Built in 1764-6, this is the oldest public building in continuous use in Manhattan. George Washington

An eternal symbol of the American dream, Eiffel's Statue of Liberty towers over New York Harbor, welcoming the people of the world

worshipped here and his private pew, in the north aisle, is the biggest attraction (tel: 602 0872).
Open: daily 07.00-16.00hrs. Tours by appointment.
Subway: Fulton Street/ Broadway.

◆◆◆
STATUE OF LIBERTY
AND ELLIS ISLAND ✓

The Statue of Liberty, a gift from the people of France, has been a national landmark in New York Harbor for more than 100 years. Sculpturing by Frenchman Frederic Auguste Bartholdi was begun in 1874 to a design engineered by Gustave Eiffel; in fact, her face is said to be that of Bartholdi's mother. The unveiling of the statue took place 12 years later and Liberty was completely refurbished for her Centennial celebrations in 1986. The statue draws the huddled masses, so expect to spend most of the morning queuing for the ferry over to Liberty Island and for the minuscule two-person lift from the ground floor to the observation deck halfway up. From here there are 168 steps up to the crown, though if you suffer from vertigo you may be content with reading the famous quote 'Give me your tired, your poor...' engraved on the base. From Liberty Island a ferry takes you on to Ellis Island and the **Immigration Museum**. Now fully restored and open to the public, the main building was once the entry point for more than 11

Grand Central Terminal is a major station and National Landmark

million immigrants from 1892 to 1954 and its museum tells the moving tales of those who entered America through the Ellis Island processing centre. There are two theatres, a learning centre and more than 30 galleries filled with artefacts, photographs, maps and posters. Access to both monuments from Battery Park by Circle Line boat (tel: 269 5755) every ½ hour from 09.30-15.00 hrs.
Open: daily 09.30-17.30hrs in summer; until 17.00 in winter.
Subway: South Ferry.

TRINITY CHURCH
74 Trinity Place at Broadway/ Wall Street
Affectionately labelled the Empire State Building of the mid-19th century, this is a gothic giant, in its day the highest rise of the city. The present building is the third construction attempt: Mark I was struck by fire, Mark II razed to the ground. As well as the regular Sunday congregation and Tuesday music recitals, the cemetery attracts its fair share of weekday sun worshippers from the surrounding office blocks.
Open: daily. Guided tours (including St Paul's Chapel, tel: 602 0872). Free.
Subway: Wall Street/Broadway.

Halls

CARNEGIE HALL
154 West 57th Street at Seventh Avenue
Dating from 1891, this is the grand old dame of opera and concert venues, which has witnessed performances by the likes of Judy Garland, Frank Sinatra and Toscanini (tel: 247 7800).
Open: 45-minute tour and film, Monday, Tuesday and Thursday at 11.30, 14.00 and 15.00hrs.
Subway: Seventh Avenue/57th Street.

GRAND CENTRAL TERMINAL

Park Avenue at 42nd Street
A National Landmark since 1978, when its fine Renaissance lines narrowly escaped demolition, and worth a look even if you're not joining the thousands of daily commuters rushing for a train. Inside it's far cleaner than many other equivalents considering it's served by more than 550 trains daily. The main concourse, in particular, is like a grand covered piazza. Underneath the clock, famous for its sculpted figures of Mercury, Athena and Hercules, is a favourite rendezvous spot for New Yorkers. The Oyster Bar (see **Food and Drink**, page 68–9) downstairs is one of the city's best restaurants. The station is open 06.00-02.00hrs and for free tours on Wednesdays at 12.30hrs (tel: 935 3960).

JACOB K JAVITS CONVENTION CENTER
655 West 34th Street
Designed by I M Pei, it has been nicknamed the Crystal Palace on account of its dramatic glass cube structure in black chrome and tinted glass, which reflects the New York skyline by day, becoming transparent by night.

Jacob K Javits Convention Center – a hi-tech crystal palace

It is considered by many to be one of the most stunning architectural achievements of the 1980s. Its space-age proportions surround a 15-storey atrium capable of holding the Statue of Liberty, or two 747 jets; while its three halls are as big as 15 American football pitches with the Galleria/River pavilion overlooking the Hudson. It is the third largest convention and trade show centre of its kind in the US and can hold 85,000 people (tel: 216 2000). *Subway:* 34th Street/Eighth Avenue.

Houses and Mansions

◆
COOPER-HEWITT
2 East 91st Street and Fifth Avenue
Andrew Carnegie's old mansion is now related to the Smithsonian Institution; the emphasis throughout its three plain but airy floors is on design (tel: 860 6868).
Open: Tuesday 10.00-21.00hrs; Wednesday to Saturday 10.00-17.00hrs; Sunday 12.00-17.00hrs. Free admission on Tuesdays, 17.00-21.00hrs. *Subway:* Lexington Avenue/86th Street.

◆◆◆
FRICK COLLECTION
1 East 70th Street
The mostly sombre collection of paintings, sculpture and decorative works from the 14th to 19th centuries is a local favourite, housed in the old Henry C Frick mansion in Fifth Avenue. An impressive array of French impressionists (tel: 288 0700).

Open: Tuesday to Saturday 10.00-18.00hrs; Sunday 13.00-18.00hrs. Introductory talks Tuesday to Friday 11.00hrs. *Subway:* Lexington Avenue/68th Street.

◆◆
GRACIE MANSION
Carl Schurz Park, East End Avenue at 88th Street
The mayor's official residence is situated in Carl Schurz Park, a tiny green breathing space above FDR Drive with views over the turbulent currents of Hell Gate on the East River. It was first opened to the public by Mayor Koch. Tours of the house, which contains many period items on loan from private collections as well as the permanent 'Merchants to Mayors' exhibition in the basement, are held on Wednesdays from March to November at 10.00, 11.00, 13.00 and 14.00hrs (tel: 570 4751 for an appointment). *Subway:* Lexington Avenue/86th Street.

◆◆◆
NEW YORK
PUBLIC LIBRARY ✓

Fifth Avenue and 42nd Street
Outside it's a beautiful Beaux Arts white marble frontage, whose entrance rivals the Spanish Steps in Rome for lounging youth. Filed inside is a book collection that ranks among the five largest in the world. There are, for example, over six million volumes in the research section. Free tours are available Monday to Saturday at 11.00 and 14.00hrs, though you can also look around on your own. The Reading Room, where Trotsky studied just before the 1917 Revolution, is the star attraction (tel: 869 8089). *Open:* Tuesday, Wednesday 11.00-18.00hrs; Thursday to Saturday 10.00-18.00hrs. *Subway:* 42nd Street/Grand Central Terminal.

Museums and Galleries
The Louvre, Tate and Uffizi pale into insignificance beside New York's art collections, and that's before you even step inside a museum. Both browsers and buyers are welcome in nearly 500 retail galleries, the main clusters being along Madison Avenue, 57th Street, Greenwich Village and around half gathered in SoHo, home of the highest concentration of avant garde art in the world. Famous names like the Marlborough, Brewster and Knoedler galleries, indicating the priciest and most exclusive works of art, can be found along Upper Madison Avenue and its opulent side streets between the 60s and 90s. The giants among Manhattan's many museums are concentrated along Museum Mile, a stretch of Fifth Avenue from 81st to 103rd Streets. Though not free, several operate a 'pay anything as long as it's something' voluntary contribution scheme, and many open one evening a week free of charge.

◆
AMERICAN MUSEUM OF THE MOVING IMAGE
35th Avenue at 36th Street, Astoria, Queens
If you have ever wondered what the key grip, best boy and

WHAT TO SEE

gaffer do on a movie set, you will find the answers here. The museum is part of the Kaufman-Astoria Studios, once occupied by Paramount Pictures for silent films and early talkies. Ghosts from the past include the Marx Brothers, Laurence Olivier, Paul Robeson, Ginger Rogers, Noël Coward, Gloria Swanson and Rudolph Valentino. More recent films made here include *Brighton Beach Memoirs*, Woody Allen's *Radio Days* and *The Cotton Club*. Exhibits range from Edison's first moving picture film camera to the newest Sony Video Walkman. Visitors can also try their hands at mixing up a soundtrack and dress up in a *Star Trek* uniform (tel: 718 784 0077).
Open: Tuesday to Friday 12.00-16.00hrs; weekends, 12.00-18.00hrs.
Subway: Steinway Street.

AMERICAN MUSEUM OF NATURAL HISTORY
Central Park West at 79th Street
The largest museum of its kind in the world, covering four blocks and containing nearly 40 million items relating to the history of animal life so don't attempt to see it all at once. Within the building are Halls of Earth History, Ocean Life, Mollusks and Mankind, Biology of Invertebrates, American Indians, Dinosaurs, Birds and Mammals, Reptiles and Amphibians, Minerals, Gems and Meteorites (tel: 769 5800).
The Hayden Planetarium, next door, holds popular late-night laser shows on Friday and Saturday (tel: 769 5921).

Open: Museum daily 10.00-17.45hrs; Friday and Saturday until 20.45hrs. Free 17.00-21.00hrs Friday and Saturday. For Planetarium times tel: 769 5100.
Subway: Central Park West/81st.

BROOKLYN MUSEUM
200 Eastern Parkway, Brooklyn
World famous for its Egyptology collection as well as impressive Roman art, photography and lithographs, and 28 period rooms. The sculpture garden is delightful (tel: 718 638 5000).
Open: Wednesday to Sunday 10.00-17.00hrs.
Subway: Eastern Parkway/ Brooklyn Museum.

THE CLOISTERS
Fort Tryon Park, Washington Heights
A branch of the Metropolitan Museum of Art, devoted to Medieval Art and blissfully removed from the freneticisim of downtown New York. Its tapestries, sculptures and other works are displayed in a European monastic setting, including parts of several medieval monasteries and chapels that were shipped over from Europe and rebuilt by enthusiastic collectors George Grey Barnard and John D Rockefeller in the early 20th century. Beautiful setting in Fort Tryon Park (tel: 923 3700).
Open: Tuesday to Sunday 09.30-17.15hrs March to October (rest of year 16.45hrs). Free tours 15.00hrs, Tuesday to Thursday. Lectures Saturday afternoon.
Subway: Fort Washington Avenue /181st Street.

◆
EL MUSEO DEL BARRIO
1230 Fifth Avenue at 104th Street
A good place to familiarise yourself with Latin American art and culture, the better to understand Spanish Harlem, where the museum stands (tel: 831 7272).
Open: Wednesday to Sunday 11.00-17.00hrs.
Subway: Lexington Avenue/ 103rd Street.

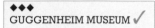

◆◆◆
GUGGENHEIM MUSEUM ✓

1071 Fifth Avenue at 88/89th Streets
The Frank Lloyd Wright-

Frank Lloyd Wright's spiralling corridor: the Guggenheim Museum, the building is a work of art in its own right

designed white concrete spiral structure a landmark in its own right has been likened to everything from a parking lot to a bee hive. Inside, a single corridor winds from ceiling to floor on a journey through Solomon Guggenheim's collection of paintings and many subsequent acquisitions. The museum, recently renovated, includes four new galleries (tel: 423 3500).
Open: Friday to Wednesday 10.00-20.00hrs (closed Thursday).
Subway: Lexington Avenue/86th Street.

◆
INTERNATIONAL CENTER OF PHOTOGRAPHY
1130 Fifth Avenue at 94th Street
When you have seen MOMA's (Museum of Modern Art – see

WHAT TO SEE

page 36) collection of photographs you can complete your education through the lenses of Cartier-Bresson, Eugene Smith, Ansel Adams and other greats. Robert Capa's brother opened this excellent centre for permanent and temporary exhibitions.
Open: Wednesday to Sunday 11.00-18.00hrs; Tuesday 11.00 until 20.00hrs. Tuesdays, free after 17.00hrs.
Subway: Lexington Avenue/96th Street.

◆
INTREPID SEA-AIR – SPACE MUSEUM
Pier 86 on the Hudson at the foot of West 46th Street
A museum of naval history and technology housed in a 900-foot (270m) World War II converted aircraft carrier.
It includes exhibits of the pioneers of aviation and films of World War II (tel: 245 0072).
Open: daily in summer; Wednesday to Sunday 10.00-17.00hrs in winter.
Subway: Fulton/William Street.

◆
JACQUES MARCHAIS CENTER OF TIBETAN ART
338 Lighthouse Avenue, Staten Island
A hilltop, temple-like museum once visited by the Dalai Lama which now contains the largest private collection of Tibetan Art in the West. Artefacts and artworks from Japan, Nepal, China, India and Southeast Asia, plus more than 1,000 volumes on Oriental philosophy, art and history.

Open: Wednesday to Sunday April to November: hours vary (tel: 718 987 3500 to check). Reached by Staten Island Ferry from southern Manhattan.

◆
JEWISH MUSEUM
109 Fifth Avenue at 92nd Street.
Recently renovated, the museum displays mainly historical ceremonial objects, from circumcision instruments to wedding rings, Torah headpieces to amulets. Elsewhere are folk art objects, exhibitions portraying the painful poverty of Lower East Side immigrants, and reminders of the Holocaust (tel: 423 3271).
Open: Monday, Wednesday, Thursday 12.00-17.00hrs, Tuesday until 21.00hrs; Sunday 11.00-18.00hrs.
Subway: Lexington Avenue/96th Street.

◆
LOWER EAST SIDE TENEMENT MUSEUM
97 Orchard Street
One in every seven Americans has roots in the Lower East Side. The museum is devoted to the hundreds of harsh, cramped, rat-infested houses endured by many Jewish immigrants from Eastern Europe at the turn of the century. There are exhibitions, dramatisations and walking tours of the area (tel: 431 0233).
Open: Tuesday to Friday 11.00-16.00hrs, Sunday 10.00-17.00hrs.
Subway: Second Avenue/Houston.

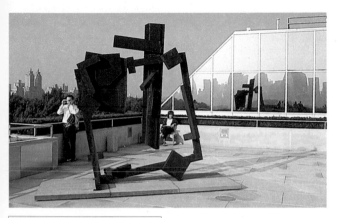

Offering a tour de force of art history, the Metropolitan Museum of Art overlooks Central Park

◆◆◆
METROPOLITAN MUSEUM OF ART ✓

1000 Fifth Avenue at 82nd Street
Despite the Met's traditional neglect of contemporary works, a new wing devoted to 20th century art has virtually doubled the city's current space devoted to modern works. It is the largest museum in the western hemisphere, extending the length of four city blocks and housing more than three million works of art. Its gargantuan exhibition space can be roughly divided into five major collections: American Painting (housed in I M Pei's wing and of particular interest to visitors from abroad), European Painting, Primitive Art (in the Michael C Rockefeller Wing), Medieval Art and Egyptian Antiquities. Exhibits date from the year dot, including classics by Rembrandt, Renoir, Velasquez, Monet, Manet and others. The sculpture garden on the roof overlooking Central Park could alone make a

pleasant morning. The museum is well-organised and provides numerous visitor services including gift shops, a café and a restaurant (tel: 535 7710).
Open: Tuesday to Thursday and Sunday 09.30-17.15hrs; Friday and Saturday until 20.45hrs. Free one-hour guided tours daily. Ticket price includes admission to Cloisters.
Subway: Lexington Avenue/77th Street.

◆
MUSEUM OF AMERICAN FOLK ART/EVA AND MORRIS FELD GALLERY

West 53rd Street
Exhibitions of handicrafts by often unknown but talented craftspeople of North, South and Central America – from run-of-the-mill ceramics to more unusual carved wooden saints (tel: 595 9533). Free.
Open: Tuesday to Sunday 11.30–19.30hrs.
Subway: Broadway/66th Street.

WHAT TO SEE

◆◆
MUSEUM OF THE AMERICAN INDIAN
part of the Audubon Terrace complex on Broadway at 155th Street

The largest gathering of Native American artifacts in the US, the collections of the Museum of the American Indian are in the process of becoming part of the Smithsonian Institution in Washington DC. A good number of the items are staying in New York, however, to form a permanent exhibition inside the former US Custom House (tel: 283 2420).
Open: Tuesday to Saturday 10.00-17.00hrs, Sunday 13.00-17.00hrs.

Contemporary movements in the Museum of Modern Art, now housed on six levels

Subway: Broadway/157th Street

◆
MUSEUM OF THE CITY OF NEW YORK
Fifth Avenue at 103rd Street

Tells the history of the Big Apple from Nieuw Amsterdam, through the sale of Manhattan for $24 to the present (tel: 534 1672).
Open: Wednesday to Saturday 10.00-17.00hrs, Sunday 13.00-17.00hrs. Tours by arrangement (tel: 534 1672 ext 206). Free.
Subway: Lexington Avenue/103rd Street.

◆◆◆
MUSEUM OF MODERN ART ✓

11 West 53rd Street

Devoted to 19th- and 20th-century art, MOMA was first established in 1929 on a donation of eight prints and one drawing. It moved to its present site in 1939, then underwent extensive rejuvenation in the '80s, when it acquired a number of steel pipe and glass extensions and an apartment building on its roof. Now there are six levels of paintings and sculptures, architecture and design (third floor), prints and illustrated books and photography. Van Gogh, Monet, Gaugin and Cezanne are on the first and second floors and don't miss the Abby Aldrich Rockefeller Sculpture Garden, with works by Moore, Picasso, Matisse and others (tel: 708 9480).
Open: Saturday-Tuesday 11.00-18.00hrs; Thursday and Friday noon–20.30hrs; closed

Wednesday. On Thursdays (after 17.00) pay what you wish.
Subway: Fifth Avenue/53rd Street.

◆

NEW YORK HALL OF SCIENCE

47-51 111th Street at 48th Avenue, Flushing Meadow Corona Park, Queens
Find out why cat's eyes glow in the dark, why the sky is blue and what makes electricity. Four ongoing major exhibitions in a 22-acre (9-hectare) site in Flushing Meadow Park, Queens (tel: 718 699 0005).
Open: Wednesday to Sunday, 10.00-17.00hrs.
Subway: Main Street/Flushing.

◆

SNUG HARBOR CULTURAL CENTER

1000 Richmond Terrace, Staten Island
America's first home for retired sailors. It's now a National Historic Landmark, an 83-acre (33.5-hectare) cultural centre for the performing and visual arts. Twenty-eight buildings, including Newhouse Center for Contemporary Art and a children's museum (tel: 718 448 2500).
Open: daily, 08.00hrs-dusk. Free tours at weekends at 14.00hrs.

◆◆◆

WHITNEY MUSEUM OF AMERICAN ART

945 Madison Avenue and 75th Street
Don't be deceived by the dreary grey façade – inside is the most avant garde of all the big league galleries with an important biennial of contemporary art, a maze of huge rooms filled with great works. The museum's collection are comprised of more than 10,000 works (drawings, sculpture, paintings and films) by famous 20th-century artists. There are also Whitney exhibitions in the Philip Morris building at 120 Park Avenue.
Open: Wednesday 11.00-18.00hrs; Thursday 13.00-20.00hrs; Friday to Sunday 11.00–18.00hrs. Free on Thursday 18.00-20.00hrs.
Subway: Lexington Avenue/77th Street.

Parks and Gardens

◆◆

BROOKLYN BOTANIC GARDEN

1000 Washington Avenue, opposite Prospect Park, Brooklyn.
Next door to the Brooklyn Museum, 52 acres (21 hectares) devoted to herbs, fragrances, Japanese, Elizabethan and other 'themes'. In the Shakespeare garden you are surrounded by flowers mentioned by the bard from Pillow Talk to Sweet Nothing. But the most famous are the three Japanese Gardens, containing the biggest collection of bonsai trees in America. Still on an Oriental theme, there are also rows of flowering pink cherry trees, a Fragrance Garden for the Blind, a Rose Garden, Herb Garden and Children's Garden, as well as the new Steinhardt Conservatory of tropical and desert plants (tel: 718 622 4433).
Open: Tuesday to Friday 08.00-18.00hrs; weekends and

WHAT TO SEE

holidays 10.00-18.00hrs, but hours vary with the seasons. Grounds and conservatory are free; small admission charge for the Japanese Gardens.
Subway: numbers 2, 3 and 4 to Prospect Park.

◆◆◆
CENTRAL PARK ✓

For the four million apartment dwellers denied all trace of rural life, Central Park is a godsend. This 840-acre, (340-hectare), two-and-a-half-mile (4km)-long back garden is (other than the weather) the only indication to many New Yorkers that the seasons are changing, and is full at weekends of people doing their particular thing.
The park was designed by Frederick Law Olmsted and Calvert Vaux, who finished it in 1876 to such acclaim that they went on to design Riverside Park and Morningside as well as Prospect Park in Brooklyn before being snapped up by the rest of the US.
For the park rangers, who wear Smokey the Bear hats, like their National Park counterparts, it is an ecological wilderness. To some it will seem a bit patchy, flowerless, overcrowded and full of the fragrances of dogs. But mock it at your peril. It is the centre for urban frustrations to erupt at weekends into jogging, cycling, skateboarding, horse-riding, roller-disco-practising, volleyballing, boat-rowing, frisbee-ing, African drumming, miming, winter skiing or skating (in Wollman Rink, restored as a result of Donald Trump's financial support), picnicking,

horse-and-carriage-riding, zoo-going, tennis-playing, pretzel or horse chestnut-munching, 'comfort station' visiting, kissing and cuddling, harmful and harmless drug taking and anything else you can imagine. Other, more tangible sights include a **Zoo** (see page 105); the Visitors Centre in **The Dairy,** a mock gothic ranch, originally built as a place for mothers to nurse their babies (open: Tuesday to Sunday, 11.00–17.00hrs, Friday from 13.00); and **Strawberry Fields,** an area dedicated to John Lennon by Yoko Ono, with trees and shrubs donated by countries around the globe.
On summer Sundays the park is the perfect place to be if you simply want to wander around like a sponge, absorbing the city at play. Bicycle hire is available from the 72nd Street boathouse. The buildings flanking the east and west sides of the park, and the many signposts, make it hard to loose your bearings completely, but losing your way temporarily is surprisingly easy. This can be especially unnerving – and dangerous – late in the day when dusk is about to fall. Make sure you have one of the maps distributed at park entrances and at the Dairy. The park's numerous isolated sections should be approached with caution and avoided completely by anyone on their own; women alone should be cautious everywhere. Entering Central Park on foot after dark is illegal.
The park runs from 59th to 110th Streets, between Fifth Avenue and Central Park West.

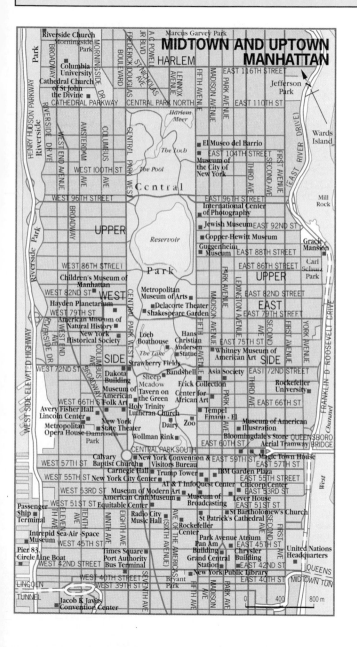

MIDTOWN AND UPTOWN MANHATTAN

Riverside Church
Morningside Park
Columbia University
Cathedral Church of St John the Divine
HENRY HUDSON PARKWAY
Riverside
RIVERSIDE DR
BROADWAY
MORNINGSIDE DR
FREDERICK DOUGLASS BLVD
A C POWELL JR BLVD
Marcus Garvey Park
HARLEM
ST NICHOLAS AVE
LENNOX AVENUE
FIFTH AVENUE
MADISON AVENUE
PARK AVENUE
EAST 116TH STREET
Jefferson Park
Wards Island
Park
CATHEDRAL PARKWAY
CENTRAL PARK NORTH
EAST 110TH ST
AMSTERDAM
COLUMBUS AVE
WEST 100TH ST
WEST 96TH STREET
CENTRAL PARK WEST
Harlem Meer
The Loch
The Pool
Central
EAST RIVER DRIVE
El Museo del Barrio
EAST 104TH STREET
Museum of the City of New York
FIRST AVENUE
SECOND AVE
THIRD AVE
EAST 96TH STREET
Mill Rock
UPPER
Reservoir
Park
WEST END AVENUE
NINTH AVE
BROADWAY
WEST 86TH STREET
Children's Museum of Manhattan
WEST 82ND ST
Hayden Planetarium
WEST 79TH ST
American Museum of Natural History
New York Historical Society
WEST SIDE ELEVATED HIGHWAY
RIVERSIDE DR
WEST END AVE
AMSTERDAM AVE
COLUMBUS AVE
CENTRAL PARK WEST
WEST 72ND ST
Dakota Building
Museum of American Folk Art
WEST 66TH ST
Avery Fisher Hall
Lincoln Center
Metropolitan Opera House
BROADWAY
Metropolitan Museum of Arts
Delacorte Theater
Shakespeare Garden
Loeb Boathouse
The Lake
Strawberry Fields
Sheep Meadow
Tavern on the Green
Dairy
Wollman Rink
Damrosch Park
MADISON AVENUE
FIFTH AVE
LEXINGTON AVENUE
PARK AVENUE
THIRD AVE
SECOND AVE
FIRST AVENUE
YORK AVENUE
EAST 92ND ST
International Center of Photography
Jewish Museum
Copper-Hewitt Museum
Guggenheim Museum
EAST 88TH STREET
EAST 86TH STREET
EAST 82ND STREET
EAST 79TH STREET
Hans Christian Andersen Statue
Whitney Museum of American Art
EAST 75TH ST
Asia Society
Bandshell
Frick Collection
Center for African Art
Holy Trinity Lutheran Church
Tempel Emann El
Zoo
New York State Theater
Gracie Mansion
Carl Schurz Park
UPPER
EAST
SIDE
EAST 72ND STREET
Rockefeller University
EAST 66TH ST
FRANKLIN D ROOSEVELT DRIVE
Channel
Museum of American Illustration
Bloomingdale's Store
Aerial Tramway
QUEENSBORO BRIDGE
CENTRAL PARK SOUTH
EAST 60TH ST
Calvary Baptist Church
WEST 57TH ST
Carnegie Hall
New York City Center
WEST 55TH ST
WEST 53RD ST
Museum of Modern Art
American Craft Museum
Equitable Center
New York Convention & Visitors Bureau
EAST 59TH ST
Magic Town House
EAST 57TH ST
Trump Tower
IBM Garden Plaza
EAST 55TH STREET
AT & T InfoQuest Center
Chicorp Center
Museum of Broadcasting
EAST 53RD ST
Lever House
Passenger Ship Terminal
Intrepid Sea-Air Space Museum
Pier 83, Circle Line Boat
TWELFTH AVE
ELEVENTH AVE
TENTH AVE
NINTH AVE
EIGHTH AVE
AVE OF THE AMERICAS (SIXTH AVENUE)
SEVENTH AVENUE
WEST 51ST ST
Radio City Music Hall
Rockefeller Center
WEST 45TH ST
Times Square
Port Authority Bus Terminal
WEST 42ND STREET
WEST 40TH STREET
WEST 39TH STREET
St Patrick's Cathedral
St Bartholomew's Church
Park Avenue Atrium
Pan Am Building
Grand Central Station
New York Public Library
EAST 42ND ST
EAST 40TH ST
Bryant Park
FIFTH AVE
MADISON AVE
PARK AVE
SECOND AVE
FIRST AVE
United Nations Headquarters
QUEENS
MIDTOWN TUN
Chrysler Building
West
LINCOLN
TUNNEL
Jacob K Javits Convention Center

0   400   800 m

WHAT TO SEE

New Yorkers in Central Park

NEW YORK BOTANICAL GARDEN

Southern Boulevard, 200th Street, North Central Bronx

One of the largest of its kind in the world. The 250-acre (100-hectare) grounds include 40 acres (16 hectares) of the original uncut forest, about the wildest natural sight you will see in the city. Don't miss the Conservatory, a leaded glass greenhouse, centrepiece of a group of 10. The Botanical Garden is part of the Bronx Zoo complex (tel: 817 8700).

Open: grounds, daily 10.00-19.00hrs, April to October (until 18.00hrs rest of year). Conservatory, Tuesday to Sunday 10.00-16.00hrs (closed Mondays). Grounds free; conservatory free on Saturdays, 10.00-12.00hrs.

PROSPECT PARK

Brooklyn

Designed by Frederick Law Olmstead, better known as the creator of Central Park across the water. Further removed from the intrusion of skyscrapers, Prospect Park is a more rural sanctuary for walking, horse-riding (stables on Caton Place), paddle-boating and bicycling. There is a zoo, also Leffert's Homestead, a Dutch Colonial structure, now a museum (*open* Wednesday to Saturday, 10.00-16.00hrs, weekends only November to March). Call at the boathouse for maps and park information (tel: 718 788 0055).

Subway: Prospect Park.

Plazas and Squares

◆◆
BATTERY PARK CITY

The newest section of Manhattan, developed on landfill from the World Trade Center, is Battery Park City, dominated by the subtle architecture of the World Financial Center. Apart from offices it houses two floors of 'upscale' shops and an enormous Winter Garden conservatory with sky-high palm tree implants that look as incongruous as skyscrapers in the Sahara. The nicest aspect of

the development are the waterside walkways, which will eventually lead all the way up the Hudson, past the largely extinct berths where the great transatlantic ships docked (and where the *QEII* and several cruiseliners still do) to Riverside Park
Subway: World Trade Center.

CASTLE CLINTON

Within grassy Battery Park proper, this is a national monument whose reincarnations have included an aquarium, immigrant landing depot, concert hall and fort. Boats leave from Battery Park to Ellis Island (the former immigration-processing centre), Liberty Island (home of the Statue), Staten Island and Governors Island (by appointment only).
Open. daily 08.30-17.00hrs; longer hours during the summer. Free admission.
Subway: South Ferry.

MADISON SQUARE GARDEN

4 Penn Plaza, Seventh Avenue, between 31st and 33rd Streets
Thrown up in 1968 amidst cries of revolt at the destruction of Pennsylvania Station. Now commuters use Penn Station underneath the building while the none-too-special upstairs is the venue for Knicks basketball and Rangers hockey matches, circuses, animal competitions and ice shows, major rock concerts and bowling (tel: 465 6000).
Subway: Penn Station.

SOUTH STREET SEAPORT

on East River, foot of Fulton Street
For a hundred years New York's port sprawled around the foot of Manhattan, beside Robert Fulton's ferry service to Brooklyn.
Now the 19th-century warehouses have undergone a facelift. Though a little too 'theme-park' for many tastes, it has an interesting collection of historic ships, a couple of real chandleries, lots of interesting shops on restored Pier 17 and two good fish restaurants: Sloppy Louie's at 92 South Street and Sweet's at 2 Fulton Street, both of which put to tasty use the morning catch from the Fulton Fish Market opposite.
The **South Street Seaport Museum**, 207 Front Street (open daily 10.00-17.00hrs, under-4's free) features changing exhibits including a children's center. All tickets include a visit to the various ships which are on display, three tours and also two films of the area. (Tel: 669 9400/9424).
Subway: Fulton/William Street.

TIMES SQUARE

at the intersection of Broadway and Seventh Avenue, between 42nd and 47th Streets
The neon-lit centrepoint of the 'Great White Way' (Broadway) is notorious for its sleazy maelstrom of theatres, movie houses, billboards and mostly tacky shops. The square was named for the *New York Times* newspaper, which built offices

WHAT TO SEE

here in 1904 but which has now sensibly escaped around the corner to 43rd Street. During the day it's only worth stopping here to queue for half-price theatre tickets at the TKTS stall, appropriately close to the statue of George M 'Give My Regards to Broadway' Cohen. By night, as long as you are careful, come to see a superb show of lights. From street level you will strain your neck; otherwise, climb to The View restaurant in the Marriot Marquis hotel, the only revolving restaurant in the city. Tel: 963 7713.
Subway: Times Square.

Skyscrapers and Landmarks

◆◆
CHRYSLER BUILDING
405 Lexington Avenue and 42nd Street
A superb example of late 20s art deco architecture, easily spotted due to its unusual, scaled spire. It was the world's tallest building for just one year, overtaken by the Empire State Building in 1931. Chrysler are no longer in residence and visitors can only stand in the lobby, though that is no pale substitute, with its African marble walls and ceiling depicting murals of the workers constructing the spire (tel: 682 3070).
Open: daily 09.00-17.00hrs.
Subway: Grand Central Terminal.

◆
CITICORP CENTER
53rd Street at Lexington Avenue
Among the more recent arrivals on the cityscape (1979)

it contains, surprisingly, the church of St Peter's, as well as one of the best atriums in town. It's known as 'The Market', a triple level mall of shops and restaurants. Topping it all is an instantly recognisable 45-degree solar panelled roof, which didn't work and now serves only as a gesture to the sky (tel: 559 2330).
Open: daily 08.00-24.00hrs.
Subway: Lexington Avenue/51st.

◆
CITY HALL
City Hall Park, Broadway and Murray Street
The acceptable face of bureaucracy, this half French château, half American Georgian building has a spiral staircase to the governor's room, surprisingly modest considering its importance (tel: 566 5700).
Open: Monday to Friday 10.00-15.30hrs. Free admission.
Subway: City Hall/Broadway

◆◆◆
EMPIRE STATE BUILDING ✓

Fifth Avenue at 34th Street
King Kong clung to it; a 1945 plane crashed into it and people have parachuted off it. This magnificent 1,454-foot (443m) art deco structure of steel, limestone and aluminium on Fifth Avenue has been open for views over the Manhattan skyline since 1931, although its main function is as an office block.
If you don't suffer from vertigo, put the city in perspective from a suitable vantage point as soon as you arrive. The Empire

State Building is favourite, although the twin towers of the World Trade Center put it in the shade. Sky-high observatories in the Empire State are open to the public on the 86th and 102nd floors, but be prepared for snaking queues of up to 30 minutes or more for the lift in summer. A single lift from the 86th floor goes 16 storeys higher, to the foot of the TV mast, but you cannot step outside (tel: 736 3100).
Open: daily 09.30-24.00hrs (last admission 23.30hrs).
Subway: Sixth Avenue/34th Street.

◆

FLATIRON BUILDING
175 Fifth Avenue at East 23rd Street
There had to be a first skyscraper and this was it, sitting on the southern flank of Madison Square; 20 storeys counted for a lot in the '20s. It was overtaken by the Metropolitan Life Company clock tower on the east side of the square. Open to the public in business hours.
Subway: Sixth Avenue/23rd Street.

◆

FRAUNCES TAVERN
54 Pearl Street at Broad Street
Deep in the heart of New York's old, hard-working commercial district, this is a 1920s reconstruction of the inn where Washington delivered his farewell address to his officers on 4 December 1783 (a shade premature since he was to return as President six years later). The restaurant is as snug

The 1,454-foot (443m) Empire State Building affords office workers and visitors rooms with a view

as a Gentleman's Club, while Washington's teeth and hair are among the displays in the museum upstairs which is devoted to the War of Independence (tel: 425 1778).
Open: Monday to Friday, 10.00-16.00hrs.
Subway: Whitehall Street/South Ferry.

◆◆

LINCOLN CENTER
Broadway and 64th Street
Hub of the performing arts in New York, this is an amalgam of six separate concert halls and theatres (including the New York State Theater and Avery Fisher Hall) and home to the New York Philharmonic,

WHAT TO SEE

the Metropolitan Opera
Company, the New York City
Opera and Ballet as well as
frequently hosting the world's
most acclaimed visiting
companies. Look out for the
huge sculpture, by Richard
Lippold, suspended in the foyer,
and Marc Chagall's murals in
the Metropolitan Opera House
(tel: 875 5400).
Open: guided tours every hour
on the hour 10.00-17.00hrs daily.
Metropolitan Opera House backstage tours, Monday to Friday at
15.45hrs; Saturday 10.00hrs.
Subway: Broadway/Lincoln
Center.

◆

The former PAN AM BUILDING
Park Avenue at East 45th Street
Previously Pan American's
headquarters and now owned
by Metropolitan Life Insurance
Company, the building was
meant to resemble an aircraft
wing, but some say it only
succeeds as a curtain, cutting
off all views along Park Avenue.
Paradoxically for the airline, the
building had a rooftop helipad
until 1977, when a helicopter
missed its footing, killing
passengers as well as others on
the ground.
Subway: Park Avenue/33rd
Street.

◆◆◆

ROCKEFELLER CENTER
*west side of Fifth Avenue, from
West 47th to 52nd Streets*
The Rockefeller family is
renowned for sparing no
expense, and this art deco
masterpiece is often referred to
as a city within a city. You could
easily disappear in here before
breakfast and not emerge till

after mid-afternoon. At the
Rockefeller's core is the GE
Building. In one corner you will
also find the restored Radio City
Music Hall, the world's largest
indoor theatre for rock concerts
and revues, including the
famous Rockettes dance troupe.
The largest chandelier in the
world hangs above the staircase,
while even the murals from the
men's toilets were considered
worthy of transferral to the
Museum of Modern Art. At the
Rockefeller Center's heart is the
Lower Plaza, a sunken garden
with a café in summer, frozen
over to form an ice rink in
winter. The Channel Gardens is
a popular space for urban flora
(tel: 698 2950/8901).
Open: RCA observation deck,
daily 09.00-17.00hrs.
Subway: Rockefeller Center.

TRUMP TOWER
Fifth Avenue at East 56th Street
Property developer and
entrepreneur Donald Trump's
best known construction,
erected in 1983 and most
famous for its pink marble
atrium, complete with shopping
centre and waterfall. Open
during business hours.
Subway: Fifth Avenue/53rd
Street.

◆◆

UNITED NATIONS
*First Avenue, between 45th and
46th Streets*
Probably best seen from the
East River on a Circle Line
cruise, 'the matchbox building',
headquarters of the United
Nations, is a distinctive
landmark on the New York
skyline. One-hour daily guided

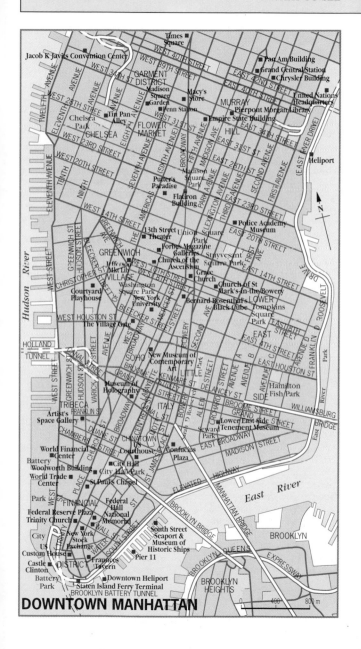

DOWNTOWN MANHATTAN

WHAT TO SEE

tours, between 09.30 and 16.45hrs, take in the Secretariat Building, General Assembly Hall, UN Craft Shop and post office, restaurants, art shows and gardens. Security concerns permitting, free tickets are issued on a first-come, first-served basis for meetings of the General Assembly shortly before 10.30 and 15.30hrs (tel: 963 7713).
Subway: Grand Central Terminal.

◆
US CUSTOM HOUSE
north of Battery Park, between Bowling Green/Bridge Street
Built in 1907 by Cass Gilbert, this granite structure is New York's grandest Beaux-Arts structure. The new US Customs Service moved site to the World Trade Center in 1973, leaving the 1907 original empty. In 1994, the Custom House is due to open with a permanent exhibition from the stocks of the Museum of the American Indian. The entrance is grand, dominated by the neo-classical style 'Four Continents' statue.
Subway: South Ferry.

◆
WOOLWORTH BUILDING
233 Broadway at Barclay Street
Much hated for its weighty gothic design; nevertheless no-one can deny that for years, in fact until the Chrysler Building was completed in 1930, this was *the* skyscraper in New York. Cass Gilbert's 1913 'Cathedral of Commerce' owes its being to the fortunes made by Frank Woolworth in his 'five and dime' stores. In fact, he paid for his building in an extraordinary cash transaction. Worth a visit

just to see the extravagant, three-storey terracotta, marble and bronze decorated lobby.
Open: daily 09.00-17.00hrs.
Subway: Park Place/Broadway.

◆◆◆
WORLD TRADE CENTER ✓

Church Street
For those who arrive by sea, the mind-boggling twin towers of the World Trade Center, glinting in the sunlight over Lower Manhattan, will be the first thing they see. For a while, they were the record holders for global height, but Chicago soon got revenge with construction of the Sears Tower.
However, the WTC towers are still tall enough to make the stomach churn at the thought of Phillip Petit's tightrope walk between the two, and George Willig's daredevil climb to the summit. Shoot up 2 WTC, the South Tower, for astounding views from the enclosed Observation Deck on the 107th floor, or up three more floors to the open air Promenade, at 1,377 feet (419m) the highest outdoor viewing platform on earth, with views far across New Jersey. Come back down and zoom up the other tower (1 WTC) for a meal at the Windows on the World restaurant.
A terrorist bomb rocked the World Trade Centre in February 1993; several people died and over 1,000 were injured. Tel: 466 7377 for general information.
Open: daily 09.30-21.30hrs (October-May); 09.30-23.30hrs (June-September).
Subway: World Trade Center.

PEACE AND QUIET

Countryside and Wildlife in and around New York

by Paul Sterry

In the midst of New York's skyscrapers and traffic, there are still pockets of comparative tranquillity, where man and wildlife live in enforced harmony. Within the city's boundaries, park woodlands and gardens can be found, together with reservoirs, lakes and swamps and the city's own wildlife refuge at Jamaica Bay. To complete the picture, journey to Long Island or south into New Jersey and you will find truly wild areas. Considering the scale of New York's urban development, the city has retained a remarkable variety of the plants, insects and mammals that would have occurred there before man's colonisation. Birds, too, are extremely varied, with over 400 species having been recorded in and around the city; the numbers of resident species and summer and winter visitors are boosted each spring and autumn by the passage migrants that pass through the region. A recorded bird alert on 832 6523, sponsored by the National Audubon Society and the Linnaen Society of New York, gives current details of unusual sightings.

In the middle of Central Park, The Lake is one of many inner-city watery attractions

PEACE AND QUIET

City Parks, Lakes and Reservoirs

New York is well endowed with parks and gardens, of which Central Park is the most famous. The park brings colour into the city with formal flowerbeds and shrubs, as well as areas of open woodland. It is home to rather dejected-looking grey squirrels, downy woodpeckers, northern flickers, black-capped chickadees and blue jays, as well as species more familiar to the European visitor: house sparrows, starlings and feral pigeons are all common. Even unusual species, such as ruby-throated hummingbirds, are occasionally seen, but it is during spring and autumn migration that Central Park, and most other parks in New York, really come into their own. After a particularly good 'fall' of migrant warblers and flycatchers, the bushes may be alive with small birds

Blue Jay (Cyanocitta cristata), a common sight in Central Park, is just one of the 400 species of birds in and around the city

searching for insects. Regularly seen species include American redstart, northern oriole, northern parula, northern waterthrush and yellow, blackpoll, palm and black-and-white warblers, but almost any species that breeds along the eastern seaboard of America may turn up.

In spring, the migrant birds are in breeding plumage and easy to spot but in autumn the range of different markings is bewildering. During September and October, particularly, New York's parks are a welcome refuge for many birds forced down by bad weather conditions. However, many fail to reach these sanctuaries, however, and their corpses can be found on the streets below the skyscrapers.

Although Central Park is well known for its birds, Forest Park in Queens, Prospect Park in Brooklyn and Pelham Bay Park in the Bronx can be equally rewarding. The lagoon in the latter park is good for waterbirds, and even Central Park's reservoir may hold great northern divers, pied-billed grebes, a variety of ducks, such as scaup and mallard, and herring, ring-billed, and occasionally laughing or glaucous gulls. Areas of swamp can be found in several places within the city, including Van Cortlandt Park in the Bronx. Wetland areas may harbour sora and Virginia rails, as well as muskrats, painted turtles, bullfrogs and water snakes and marshland plants like cattail, bur-reed and common reed, with skunk cabbage and dog-tooth violet growing under damp woodland.

Catbrier and poison ivy thrive in neglected copses, which may comprise both native trees, such as aspen, poplar and birch, and a variety of alien and exotic species. This pattern is also found among smaller plants: several species of clover, as well as perforate St John's wort and ragwort, from Europe, grow in waste places, while purple loosestrife is colonising marshes and proving a threat to native wetland species. Parks and gardens in more outlying, rural suburbs of New York often have a surprising variety of insects. During the summer months, cicadas sing from the trees and katydids crawl among the leaves. Colourful butterflies, such as tiger swallowtail, spicebush swallowtail, monarch and Camberwell beauty (mourning cloak) feed by day, while, at night, huge hawk moths and luna moths are attracted to lights. After dark, mammals like skunk, opossum and red fox venture out and are sometimes caught in car headlights.

Birds on the Hudson River

The waterfront of the mighty Hudson River is a focal point for many people's visits to New York. Over a mile (1.6km) wide at the mouth, it is large enough

Thriving in neglected copses, the famous Poison Ivy is found throughout New York's parks

PEACE AND QUIET

to be plied by ocean-going vessels. It also harbours a surprising range of birds. Whether you view from the shores of the Hudson or from boats to the Statue of Liberty or the Staten Island–Manhattan ferry, gulls will always be in evidence. Herring and ring-billed gulls are present throughout the year, with glaucous and great black-backed gulls in winter and Bonaparte's and laughing gulls in spring. The Hudson River is an important migration route for many birds and in spring and autumn, several species of terns pass through.

The Hudson River is an important wintering area for many waterbirds. Red-throated and great northern divers, cormorants and double-crested

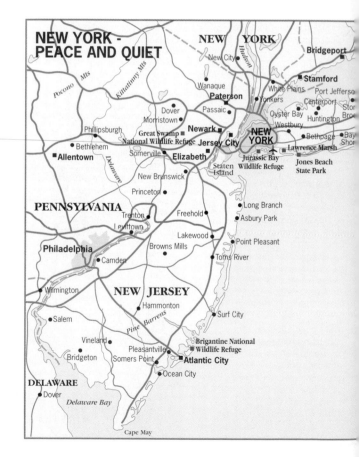

cormorants, Slavonian grebes, scaup, goldeneye, red-breasted mergansers and three species of scoter are usually present, each favouring slightly different sites.

Pelagic Trips

New York's position on the eastern seaboard of America makes it a prime place to observe some of the riches of

CONNECTICUT

New Haven

Long Island Sound

Greenport
Peconic

Orient Beach
State Park

Montauk
Point

Montauk

Riverhead

Sag Harbour

Hampton Bays

Moriches Bay

Patchogue

Long Island

Fire Island

| 0 | 20 | 40 | 60 | 80 km |

| 0 | 20 | 40 miles |

the Atlantic Ocean. During periods of onshore gales, the shores of Long Island become littered with seaweed, shells and the remains of other marine creatures, while offshore, truly oceanic birds can be seen battling against the wind. However, to get a real taste of the Atlantic, a day's boat trip out to sea is well worth the effort. Keep in mind, though that although the wildlife may be interesting, the Atlantic is seldom a welcoming destination, and you will need sea-sickness tablets and warm, weather-proof clothing.

Fishing trips operate out of most of the ports on the south of Long Island as far east as Montauk, often in search of mackerel or bluefin tuna during the summer. Non-fishermen are usually welcome, but try to pick a boat which is going well away from land: the further away, the more oceanic species you will see. From a naturalist's point of view, the seabirds are the most noticeable inhabitants of the ocean, although from time to time brown sharks and jellyfish are seen on calm days.

Herring and ring-billed gulls gradually disappear as you move further from land and species like kittiwake, gannet, great shearwater and great skua take their place.

Fishermen often spread 'chum' on the water to attract fish, but it has the added benefit of drawing in birds as well. Shearwaters, and the occasional fulmar or Sabine's gull in autumn, are often joined by considerable numbers of Wilson's petrels, which dance

Visitors to Long Island's beaches may be lucky enough to spot a horseshoe crab

over the surface of the water with feet pattering the surface. This tiny species is one of the most numerous in the world, with breeding colonies of millions of birds in the Antarctic. Thousands migrate north each year to spend the summer in the north Atlantic. Pelagic trips off Long Island regularly encounter whales, and a whale-watching tour operates out of Montauk. On calm days, their 'blows' can be seen and heard from a considerable distance, and exceptional views may be had of these gentle leviathans. Finback whales, the second largest animal ever to live, are often seen; and humpback whales, minke whales and white-sided dolphins are regular from June to August.

Long Island

Long Island's name accurately describes its terrain. It stretches west to east from New York out into the Atlantic and has more of a rural feel than the city itself. Long Island has supported farming communities and small settlements for generations,

but has more recently experienced larger scale development, with the result that few areas of habitat can now be considered truly natural. However, much of the island's coastline is comparatively unspoilt, and it lures lovers of wildlife and the outdoors from far afield. The northern half of Long Island is a landscape of rolling hills, while the southern part is flat. Around the coast, and particularly on the south of the island, harbours, sand dunes, beaches and the untamed Atlantic provide an attractive setting for birds and flowers, and many areas fall within parks or sanctuaries: Lawrence Beach, Jones Beach State Park, Orient Beach State Park and Moriches Bay are well worth visiting. Beachcombers will be delighted by the variety of natural treasures to be found on the tideline – moon shells, clams, periwinkles, starfish, sand dollars and horseshoe crabs.

Sandhoppers and kelp flies feed among the rotting seaweed and provide a meal for energetic sanderlings, while ring-billed gulls and herring gulls search for bulkier items of food. Above the high tide line, little terns, common terns, piping plovers and occasionally black skimmers make nest scrapes in the sand and gravel, which is colonised by maritime plants such as sea rocket and sea pea.

The further east on Long Island you travel, the more rural the landscape. Birds such as eastern kingbird, mourning dove, blue jay, swallow and American goldfinch are often seen perched near roads through farmland, while catbirds and mockingbirds dash between areas of cover. Woodlands, which may comprise aspens, oaks, witch-hazel, choke-cherry and flowering dogwood, provide a home for northern flickers, American redstarts and black-capped chickadees, as well as mammals like grey squirrels and chipmunks.

During the spring, but especially in autumn, the shores of Long Island swarm with migrant waders. Short-billed dowitchers, marbled godwits, lesser yellowlegs, grey plovers and willets feed alongside several smaller species. Least sandpiper, semi-palmated sandpiper and dunlin are common, and there is always a chance of finding white-rumped sandpiper or Baird's sandpiper among them. Marshland areas around the coast support common reed, reedmace and pickerel-weed, and may have breeding herons, egrets, willets and seaside sparrows, while, further inland among the dunes, bayberry bushes, poison ivy and catbrier harbour tired migrants. Ideal weather conditions for grounding migrant birds are cold fronts and northwesterly winds in autumn, after which hundreds of warblers and sparrows can be found. In late autumn and early winter, snow buntings and Ipswich sparrows can be found, while over the dunes and fields, rough-legged buzzards, short-eared owls and occasionally even snowy owls are seen.

Long Island's position in the Atlantic makes it an ideal spot from which to observe seabirds. Autumn and winter are the best seasons and Montauk Peninsula, at the far eastern tip of the island, is a particularly rewarding site. Wilson's petrels, skuas, shearwaters and gannets are seen in late summer gales, while in winter there are glaucous gulls, harlequin ducks, scoters and red-throated divers.

Jamaica Bay Wildlife Refuge

Jamaica Bay Wildlife Refuge lies in the shadow of New York, on the southern shores of Brooklyn and beneath the flight path of international jets. Despite its urban setting and the man-made nature of this wildlife haven, it has an international reputation as one of the city's natural history highlights. Several species of egrets and herons breed here during the summer months and, in spring and autumn, the resident bird population is swollen with migrants. Even winter has its highlights: thousands of wildfowl live within the refuge boundaries or just offshore, and landbirds such as Ipswich sparrow, Lapland bunting and short-eared owl can be found. Pools at Jamaica Bay are usually full of birds. Tricoloured, little-blue and green herons and great, snowy and cattle egrets breed here. Great blue herons occasionally stalk the waters along with glossy ibises, while herring, ring-billed and laughing gulls are common. Forster's and black terns stop to bathe and preen, especially in the late summer and autumn. Waders, or shorebirds, can also be abundant in spring and autumn. Lesser yellowlegs, godwits, willets, dunlins, least sandpipers and semi-palmated sandpipers are regularly seen. Although at first they may look confusingly similar, each species has its own unique appearance and a pair of binoculars and a good bird book should help you sort them out. Careful observation in the autumn may also reveal one of Jamaica Bay's more unusual visiting waders, such as white-rumped sandpiper, buff-breasted sandpiper or pectoral sandpiper.

The saltmarshes attract large numbers of brent geese in the winter, which feed on the eelgrass and stay long after the migrating Canada geese have departed. Other visiting and resident wildfowl include mallard, black duck, gadwall, green-winged teal and American wigeon. In spring the males have beautiful breeding plumage, but in summer and early autumn they moult into a drab plumage called 'eclipse'. For a few weeks each year it can be very difficult to identify individual ducks with certainty.

New Jersey

If you get weary of the hustle and bustle of city life, it might be worth considering a drive south into New Jersey. Despite widespread urban development, the coastal strip has more to offer the visiting naturalist than New York city, and the state is one of the best in eastern North America for observing autumn migration. Many good sites still exist in New Jersey, but three – Brigantine National Wildlife Refuge, Great Swamp National Wildlife Refuge and Cape May – stand out.

Brigantine NWR, near Atlantic City, is a maze of fresh water and saltmarsh. Viewed from your car, pools with egrets, herons, ibises, geese, ducks and waders can be seen, and the refuge is good throughout the year. Great Swamp NWR, near Newark, has both woodlands and marshes full of tree frogs, cattail and pickerel weed. Rails, ducks and herons haunt the marsh while warblers, flycatchers and woodpeckers favour the woodland.

Cape May is known by birdwatchers the world over,

and has given its name to one of America's most attractive warblers. Although good at all times of year, the autumn migration of birds of prey, warblers, sparrows and vireos can be spectacular.

Buffalo and Niagara Falls

Many visitors to New York make the journey upstate to the Niagara Falls. The city of Buffalo makes a good base from which to explore not only the falls but also the Niagara River, Lakes Erie and Ontario as well as the surrounding marshes and woodland.

Niagara attracts not only human visitors but birds as well: thousands of migrants pass through in spring and autumn

Sora Rail: many rails are found in the New Jersey marshes

and, because the waters are invariably ice-free, many species spend the winter here. Damp woodlands harbour grey squirrels and chipmunks as well as colourful butterflies and birds such as chickadees, red-eyed vireos and overbirds. Almost any migrant species which breeds further north in Canada may turn up in spring and autumn.

The Niagara River is the haunt of ring-billed and herring gulls as well as glaucous and Iceland gulls in winter and Bonaparte's and Franklin's gulls on migration. Wading birds can be found in shallow water or on beaches, while great northern divers, grebes and diving duck such as long-tailed duck, goldeneye and bufflehead much prefer the open water.

FOOD AND DRINK

FOOD AND DRINK

New York is a city for imbibing. There are around 17,000 restaurants, occupying 35 of Manhattan's *Yellow Pages*, plus 25,000 other eating places. The fact that New York is home to countless ethnic groups, who have re-established traditional ways in various neighbourhoods throughout the city, means that you can always find the food you crave. As long as the restaurant of your fancy hasn't suddenly been written up by Mimi Sheraton, influential food critic of the *New York Times*, or newly patronised by such Manhattan-dwelling superstars as Woody Allen, Liza Minelli or Robert de Niro, you should manage to get in and pay a reasonable price.

Ease yourself gently into the melting pot with a visit to **Zabar's** on Broadway at 80th

New York's cafés and restaurants reflect the city's style and pace

Street. King of the Upper West Side's gourmet food emporia, and open 365 days a year, it is a city landmark and the ultimate deli, its counters an excellent reflection of the cultural mish-mash out on the streets. Here you can fill your basket with Italian pastas, Russian caviars, Argentine cheeses, Brazilian coffee, Jewish bagels, German marzipan, Chinese prawns, Greek olives, French snails and English teas.

New York is a city of eating fads. The restaurant that offers the essential dining experience one week, rating almost a column in the *New York Magazine*, may well be a struggling 'has been' six months later. Silverbird's American Indian Restaurant, for example, that opened on

Columbus in 1986, required a strong stomach for its baked rattlesnake and buffalo burgers, but the critics were enthusiastic. Two years later it was no more, having caused little more than a hiccup in the city's insatiable appetite. Only the closure of the trendy Maxwell Plum on the affluent Upper East Side of town took everyone by surprise. The secret of eating well but cheaply in New York is to stick to neighbourhood cafés and delis. As long as they are full of locals, you can be sure they are good. If you want Italian, for example, head for Little Italy. Across Canal Street in Chinatown the choice of cheap but delicious meals is enormous. You can go Greek in Astoria, for example, Indian along Lexington Avenue, Jewish in the Lower East Side and Middle Eastern along Atlantic Avenue in Brooklyn.

Prices

Reckon on paying around $75 per head and upwards for dinner in the smartest, most exclusive establishments; $40-$50 in the expensive, $20-$35 in the moderate and $15 in the obviously inexpensive. A tax on your meal will be 8.25 per cent, and it is standard practice to double the tax as a tip, unless there is a 15 per cent service charge already on the bill. Not all restaurants accept credit cards, so check first to avoid embarrassment, though you can always pay in dollar travellers' cheques if they have a recognisable US trademark such as American Express or First National City. Another tip:

if you find you can not eat it all in one go, it is standard practice in America to ask for a 'doggy bag' to take the rest home, even in a fairly smart establishment.

Breakfast and Brunch

'I've never had a really good American dinner,' wrote Steinbeck. 'But then I've never had a really bad American breakfast.' There is a coffee shop or basic diner on virtually every street corner, serving breakfast specials until halfway through the morning, though you may need your dictionary for even this simple event to translate eggs 'sunnyside up' (yolk on top) or 'over easy' (flipped over once in the frying pan).

Take your fill of buckwheat pancakes, hash brown potatoes or home fries, grits, waffles, corn muffins, crispy bacon and endless refills of coffee for $10 or less.

At the weekend, relax over a brunch, usually served from noon until around 16.00hrs. It could be bagels with lox and cream cheese, savoury crêpes, red caviar and sour cream omelettes, steak and eggs or a spinach quiche, plus cocktails with Bucks Fizz usually topping the poll. Top of the expense account list for mid-week 'power brunching' are **Windows on the World**, 107th floor, 1 World Trade Center (tel: 938 1111), which can also claim to have the best wine selection in New York; **Tavern on the Green**, Central Park West and 67th Street (tel: 873 3200); **Ristorante 75**, Columbus Avenue at 67th

FOOD AND DRINK

Street; and the **Ferrybank Restaurant**, Front Street, Brooklyn. For brunch with unlimited champagne, try **Biltmore Garage**, 1 Mitchell Place/First Avenue at 49th Street (tel: 832 8558).

Cafés, Delis and Diners

Ask a hundred New Yorkers to pick their favourite diner, deli (delicatessen) or coffee shop and you would end up with a hundred different answers. Among the long-established favourites are:

Carnegie Deli, 854 Seventh Avenue at 55th Street (tel: 757 2245). Just around the corner from Carnegie Hall; famous for pickling its own gherkins and stuffing its own olives. It only closes for two and a half hours a day (04.00–06.30hrs). Huge breakfast menu delivered by gravy-stained waiters, plus the type of sandwiches you can never get your mouth around. Cash only.

Empire Diner, 210 10th Avenue at West 22nd Street (tel: 924 0011). Aspires to better (and more expensive) dishes than bacon and eggs, moving to burgers, chicken, and American dinners as the day progresses. You could almost get by just on their 'hedonist's' sandwich of the day. The art deco chrome and black polished glass decor and nostalgic music attracts the young; at night it takes the mood of a smart restaurant.

Good Enough to Eat, 424 Amsterdam Avenue near West 80th Street (tel: 496 0163). It certainly is: gigantic portions of egg, crispy bacon, blueberry muffins with strawberry butter,

spicy home fries and king-size mugs of coffee. Packed at weekends.

Hard Rock Café, 221 West 57th Street, between Broadway and Seventh Avenues (tel: 489 6565). A branch of the worldwide chain, with musical accessories which once belonged to the rich and famous mounted on the wall. Loud music to chew to and the inevitable queue on the sidewalk. But the burgers, chips and salads are as good as their reputation.

Moondance Diner, 80 Sixth Avenue at Grand Street (tel: 226 1191). Caters predominantly for the late night, post-entertainment SoHo revellers who feel like hanging out over a plate of ham 'n' eggs and a glass of champagne for a few hours more. There's more to the name than romance: you actually can dance by summer moonlight on the patio of this pre-Second World War railway carriage. Breakfasts, pancakes and lunchtime salads.

Sarabeth's, 424 Amsterdam Avenue at 80th Street (tel: 496 6280), and 1295 Madison Avenue between 92nd and 93rd Streets (tel: 410 7335). The brainchild of a lady who started making homemade jams, muffins and cookies and found that half of New York wanted to eat them. Weekend queues extend down the street – if you can't get in on Amsterdam Avenue, try the quieter branch at the **Wales Hotel** on the Upper East Side.

Second Avenue Kosher Deli, 156 Second Avenue at 10th Street (tel: 677 0606). Second by name and second only to the Carnegie Deli by nature – though its regulars would argue the point. Wholesome and Jewish in the heart of the East Village.

Spring Street Market, 111 Spring Street (tel: 226 4410). A deli, despite the name, which makes up excellent sandwiches to eat in or take away.

Fast Food

All-American steaks, hamburgers and plain meat 'n' potatoes are widely available at reasonable prices. Try **Miss Ruby's Café**, 135 Eighth Avenue at 16th Street (tel: 620 4055).

Ray's Pizza bars throughout town sell by the slice, as well as various sizes of whole, though the best in town is served at **Johns**, 408 East 64th Street (tel: 935 2895) or in its recently expanded premises at 278 Bleecker Street, between Sixth and Seventh Avenues (tel: 243 1680) and **Arturo's**, 106 West Houston Street (tel: 475 9828), cooked in coal ovens with live music most evenings. **Fiorello's Roman Café**, 1900 Broadway, between 63rd and 64th Streets (tel: 595 5330), is more than a café, less than a restaurant.

Diners – like the up-market Empire – can satisfy the eyes and the ears as well as the taste buds: good décor, good music and good food

FOOD AND DRINK

New York Magazine food critic, Gael Greene, once pronounced its pizza the best in New York, which it has been using in its advertising ever since.

Gray's Papaya fruiterias, again all over town, serve the best fresh fruit drinks in New York, all blended papaya, banana, and non-alcoholic pina coladas and daquiris in double-quick time. **Amy's** is the best chain of health and wholefood restaurants in the city; branches all over mid and uptown Manhattan.

The most ubiquitous burger chain is **Burger King**, though there are also countless **McDonald's**, as well as other American varieties. The most up-market hamburger in town comes from **P J Clarke's**, 915 Third Avenue at 55th (tel: 759 1650) served in a mostly male, wood panelled bar atmosphere.

Of the many steakhouses, try **Gallagher's**, 228 West 52nd Street (8th and Broadway) (tel: 245 5336), traditional and sporty. They will happily sell you some of the special sauce – but don't ask for the recipe, because you won't get it. **The Palm**, 837 Second Avenue, between 44th and 45th Streets (tel: 687 2953), is the steak equivalent of Maxim's and always crowded. For budget steaks you'll find it hard to beat any of the **Beefsteak Charlie's**, 1655 Broadway (tel: 757 3110). For the quintessential New York frankfurter, or frank, no-one beats **Nathan's Famous**. Nathan Handwerker started serving the seaside crowds from his Coney Island stand in 1916. There are now franchises all over town. Franks are best ordered with a tray of golden, crispy French fries.

Daytime street traders are prolific, particularly in midtown, including Fifth Avenue for hungry lunchtime shoppers. Hot dogs, pretzels and knishes are the most popular; kebabs, souvlaki and chestnuts close behind. Delis will make up a bulging pastrami (salt beef) sandwich, topped with a giant dill pickle to take away, and scores of places will make up delicious doorstep sandwiches, usually large enough for two, and offer all manner of bagels. Just for the record, a hero is a type of sandwich as well as a highly decorated war veteran; so is a sub.

Inside and out, the Hard Rock Café is known for the memorabilia mounted on its walls

Restaurants

Chinese

It is especially hard for a visitor to distinguish between the hundreds of restaurants in Chinatown, but since it's equally hard to eat a bad meal, you can take pot luck in most of them without hardship. But it's as well to remember that you will come across some shocking ingredients; look before you select.

Most Chinese restaurants fall in the moderate to inexpensive category. The biggest bargain is a lunchtime *Dim Sum* ('your heart's delight') whereby you help yourself to little dishes from a moving trolley and tot up the empties at the end.

Hee Sung Feung, 46 Bowery (tel: 374 1319) between Canal and Third Avenue, otherwise known as HSF, does an excellent version. Also at **Hong-Ying**, 11 Mott Street, **Yun Luck Rice**, 17 Doyers Street, **Non-Wah**, 13 Doyers Street and **Mon Hueng Seafood**, 18 Elizabeth Street, all big, overly lit restaurants.

Phoenix Garden, 46 Bowery Arcade, next to Elizabeth Street (tel: 962 8934). An up-market Chinese, off the beaten tourist track in a decidedly grubby arcade. However, it has earned top marks for its Cantonese dishes. Excellent value for money and a friendly choice for families.

Silver Palace, 52 Bowery (tel: 964 1204). Very popular, also for *Dim Sum*.

Szechuan Taste, 189 Bleecker Street (tel: 260 2333). One of the best of its kind in town.

Wong Kee, 113 Mott Street, near Hester Street (tel: 966 1160). Brightly lit, noisy, crowded and certainly not the place for a romantic *à deux*. But for a roll-your-sleeves-up-and-get-stuck-in cheap meal, it's unbeatable. Speciality of the house is *hong shiu* chicken, fried spring chicken on shredded bamboo, vegetables and mushrooms. Dishes come fast, so to avoid indigestion only order the next as the previous dish arrives.

French

Most French restaurants in New York are expensive, rarely offer *prix fixe* menus and do not always live up to the size of the bill. But smaller, cosy bistros are becoming more popular, predominantly in the West Village, perhaps this city's answer to yesterday's Montmartre.

Café des Artistes, 1 West 67th Street (tel: 877 3500). The *Zagat New York City Restaurant Survey*, voicing the opinion of New York's regular restaurant addicts, votes this the most romantic restaurant in town. It has an old world ambience and is famous for its nude nymph murals, and extravagant use of plants and mirrors. It also serves great brunch and desserts.

Café Un, Deux, Trois, 123 West 44th Street (tel: 354 4148). French brasserie, with crayons on the table in case you get bored between courses.

Chez Brigitte, 77 Greenwich Avenue (tel: 929 6736). A snug, homely and inexpensive refuge, run only by Brigitte

FOOD AND DRINK

and one helper; just as well, since customers are squeezed into such modest proportions that there's room for no more than 11. The place for *boeuf bourgignon*.

Chez Laurence Pâtisserie, 245 Madison Avenue at 38th Street (tel: 683 0284). The setting – the first floor of the Madison Tower Hotel – may sound uninspiring, but once inside this French café and pâtisserie, you are in La Belle France, right down to the stills from French cinema on the wall and the selection of croissants, briôches and cream-oozing pastries. Avoid the busy lunchtime period.

Eze, 254 West 23rd Street (tel: 691 1140). If you're a lover of Provençal herbs and marinades, this Chelsea townhouse, not long opened by chef-owner Gina Zarrilli, is a real find.

La Caravelle, 33 West 55th Street (tel: 586 4252). The last word in old-fashioned luxury (they still carve meat next to your table). It used to be under the influence of a powerful young chef, Michael Romano. He recently moved on and the future performances remain to be judged.

La Chanterelle, 6 Harrison Street at Hudson Street (tel: 966 6960). TriBeCa has two of the city's best French restaurants: **Bouley's** (see page 68) and **La Chanterelle**, which recently moved from SoHo in an expansion which raised the number of tables from 12 to a staggering 15. Service and setting are natural and friendly, the food *nouvelle cuisine* and

delicious. Reservations essential.

Le Côte Basque, 5 East 55th Street (tel: 688 6525). Le Pavillion, New York's first French restaurant *extraordinaire*, was open for some 30 years after its namesake at the 1939 World's Fair. It closed down in 1969 after training many of New York's top French chefs. Le Côte Basque, the heir, is still one of the best in town and among the most expensive, with exquisite dishes prepared by chef Jean-Jacques Rachou. It's popular for its murals of the French Basque coast and seafood dishes.

Le Cygne, 55 East 54th Street (tel: 759 5941). Fixed price meals, very expensive and a pleasant, if rather snooty atmosphere. But it is worth a visit just for the beautiful, flower-filled surroundings. Meals have improved since the arrival of Jean-Michel Bergougnous, formerly chef de cuisine at Lutèce.

Le Zinc, 139 Duane Street (tel: 732 1226). A TriBeCa bistro with dark wood, paddle fans and two cats almost as plush as the furnishings. Like its neighbours, it almost stands on its own as a bar. You can be sure things will liven up considerably as the evening wears on.

Lutèce, 249 East 50th Street (2nd and 3rd Avenues) (tel: 752 2225). A townhouse location in a not particularly posh area of town, but right at the top of the list of prime places to dine. It lays claim to customers who worship André

Eating out is a serious business in New York, and 'foodies' abound

Soltner's *salmon en croute, soufflé glacé* and *medallions de veau aux morilles*. They make it quite impossible for others to reserve. Closed Sundays and August.

Magic Pan Crêperie, 149 East 57th Street (tel: 371 3266). As good a selection of sweet and savoury, nourishingly filled pancakes as in any Breton crêperie.

Quatorze, 240 West 14th Street near Eighth Avenue (tel: 206 7006). A classic, wholesome French bistro tucked away in the Village. Book ahead, as its easy-going atmosphere and very reasonable menu prices make it popular and crowded.

The Terrace, 400 West 119th Street (tel: 666 9490). The area around Columbia University is not the place you would expect to find a smart restaurant serving classic Gallic fare to the strains of a harp, but The Terrace is the perfect choice for a romantic meal. It has the added bonus of excellent views of Manhattan.

Greek
The Greek restaurants in Manhattan are poor cousins of those across the river. The most authentic Greek restaurants are to be found in Brooklyn's Astoria district. In Manhattan, you could try **Delphi**, 109 West Broadway (tel: 227 0322) for cheap, filling and excellent antipasti and fish.

Italian
When New Yorkers go out to eat in the evening, their most popular choice is Italian. Most would not consider going anywhere for it but Little Italy. Home-made pastas are as superbly and lovingly rolled, simmered *al dente* or baked in this concentration of trattorias as back home in Naples or Sicily, while a cappuccino at either **Café Figaro** or **Borgia**, both on corners where

FOOD AND DRINK

Bleecker Street meets MacDougal, is the nearest New York gets to a Latin Quarter.

Angelo's, 146 Mulberry Street (tel: 966 1277). One of the best, and a Little Italy landmark, with a loyal group of fans. These include Ronald Reagan, who always eats here when in New York.

Café Pacifico, 384 Columbus (tel: 724 9187). Pasta, pasta and more pasta. The décor is completely OTT and the food can be rather expensive for what you get.

Café Trevi, 1570 First Avenue, between 81st and 82nd Streets (tel: 249 0040). Simple but delicious pasta and bottles of inexpensive but perfectly palatable wines on tables decked in check.

Cent'anni, 50 Carmine Street (tel: 989 9494). Don't go for the décor, but the cuisine, which has most customers in raptures. All the classic Italian ingredients are here on a simple menu but in flourishing form: wild mushrooms, fresh herbs, garlic and woody olive oils.

Da Silvano, 260 Sixth Avenue (tel: 982 2343). A fashionable Florentine establishment, by no means cheap, but the chic, SoHo clientele don't seem to mind.

Da Umberto, 107 West 17th Street (tel: 989 0303). Famous for its display of mouthwatering antipasti; it seems a shame to spoil it by ordering. Leave your menu to one side and ask for one of the many delicious specials.

Duane Park Café, 157 Duane Street, Hudson and West Broadway (tel: 732 5555). One of the newer establishments in TriBeCa, with a refined menu, which may start with soft shell crab, followed by seafood risotto or pan-blackened salmon and a slab of frozen Dacquoise Cake for dessert.

Francesca's, 129 East 28th Street between Lexington and Park (tel: 685 0256). A neighbourhood Italian restaurant in the East Side Midtown definition. Good food in simple surroundings and very friendly staff.

La Luna, 112 Mulberry Street (tel: 226 8657). One of the all-time eating bargains in New York. Moody waiters and rather too intimate views of the kitchen for some tastes, but the food is superb.

Mario's, 2342 Arthur Avenue

Sylvia's Restaurant proves that good food exists outside Manhattan, but no need to put on the ritz for this Harlem venue

(tel: 584 1188). The crisp tablecloths, veal cutlet parmigiano and fine wines make Mario's one of the best reasons for many New Yorkers to cross into the Bronx.
Orso, 322 West 46th Street (tel: 489 7212). Like its London namesake, this restaurant is owned by Joe Allen and is a favourite with media and theatre folk. Predominantly northern Italian cooking in an airy, white-painted plaster setting, offset by lots of colourful Mediterranean ceramics.
Palio, Equitable Center, 151 West 51st Street, at 7th Avenue (tel: 245 4850). Named after the famous annual horserace in Sienna, and there is no escaping the inspiration: the bar downstairs is surrounded by a Sandro Chia mural of the event on all four walls. Dining is fine and expensive, even described as 'the Giorgio Armani of restaurants'. Beautifully laid tables and subtly designed seasonal dishes. Don't miss the house risotto.
Pietro-Vanessa, 23 Cleveland Place (tel: 226 9764). On the fringes of Little Italy, this is one of the best of the neighbourhood Italian restaurants, with a back yard for *al fresco* dining and excellent home cooking. Still little known by most New Yorkers, let alone out-of-towners.
Positano, 250 Park Avenue South at 20th Street (tel: 777 6211). All the ingredients of the Sorrento peninsula are here, from marinaded fish dishes to the Amalfi chocolate and

almond cake that could have been flown in especially for the occasion. The customers even sit at tables on different levels, like the houses that tumble down the cliffs.
Puglia, 189 Hester Street, at Mott and Mulberry Streets (tel: 966 6006). For those wanting a lively night out: the atmosphere is noisy and cheerful and everyone sits at long trestle tables, enjoying extremely good value food.
Rosemarie's, 145 Duane Street (tel: 285 2610). A small, intimate and friendly TriBeCa eatery, that's fond of the Sandersonesque wallpaper and dried flowers image. Note, before drinking, that, of the three arches on the end wall, only one is real, the others *trompe l'oeil*. Imaginative pastas are the speciality. If you get there too early for your table or friends, you can perch at a beautiful wooden bar.
Trattoria da Alfredo, 90 Bank Street (tel: 929 4400). Immensely popular, with a reservations book filled a week or two before. Bring your own drink.
Villa Pensa, 198 Grand Street (tel: 226 8830). Family-run since 1898, and still serving delicious antipasto and home-made ravioli and manicotti.

Japanese
Sushi bars, serving exquisitely prepared, predominantly raw fish dishes, were first adopted by the brigades of yuppies, but have since broadened in appeal. The best include **Genroku Sushi**, 365 Fifth Avenue (tel: 947 7940); **Hatsuhana**, 17 East 48th Street

FOOD AND DRINK

(tel: 355 3345) and **Sakura**, 2298 Broadway (tel: 769 1003). Though *sushi* bars are mostly expensive and starkly elegant, there is a Japanese answer to McDonald's in New York: the **Dosanko** chain; and a cheap, fun and popular restaurant, **Dojo**, in the East Village: 24 St Mark's Place (tel: 674 9821).

Jewish/German/East European
Café Geiger, 208 East 86th Street (tel: 734 4428). A well-known German restaurant in Yorkville.
Katz's Deli, 205 East Houston Street (tel: 254 2246). Of 'Send a salami to your boy in the army' World War II poster fame. One of New York's prized delis on the Lower East Side, though more a restaurant than a deli.
Kleine Konditorei, 234 East 86th Street (tel: 737 7310). All the pastries, sausages and beans you can manage.
Ratner's, 138 Delancey Street (tel: 677 5588). A dairy restaurant that's always packed, even though it's quite expensive.
Veselka, 144 Second Avenue at East Ninth Street (tel: 228 9682). A glorified coffee shop, catering for those homesick for the chill winds that whip across Eastern Europe: steaming mugs of strong coffee and hand-warming bowls of soup. This is an East Village hangout, popular with the area's more bohemian residents. It also serves salad, meat, stuffed cabbage, banana wheatcakes and, surprisingly, delicious New England ice cream.

Mexican/Spanish/Regional US Alcala
US Alcala, 349 Amsterdam Avenue, between 76th and 77th Streets (tel: 769 9600). A large, noisy restaurant whose Galician owner's reputation for authentic *tapas* carries far beyond the Upper West Side location. Beautiful, marble-topped bar and delicious paella. There will soon be a backyard for summer outdoor dining.
Betty Brown's Broadway Diner, Broadway and West Houston (tel: 490 9633). Huge choice of Mexican dishes in the Village.
Café Espanol, 172 Bleecker Street (tel: 475 9230). An easy-going little restaurant in the Village, where you can sit down to a seafood and shellfish platter and other simple Spanish food.
Caramba, 918 Eighth Avenue at 54th Street (tel: 245 7910); 684 Broadway at Third Street (tel: 420 9817) and 1576 Third Avenue at 88th Street (tel: 876 8838). There are several of these rather fashionable restaurants, each with a hectic atmosphere. Great margueritas.
Cinco de Mayo, 349 West Broadway, between Broome and Grand Street (tel: 226 5255); and 45 Tudor City Place (tel: 661 5070). Supposedly celebrating the winning of a great Mexican battle, the food is rather more Tex-Mex than pure Mex and, some say, a little overrated, despite its enormous popularity.
Cottonwood Café of Manhattan, 415 Bleecker Street (tel: 924 6271). Noisy and

popular with NYU students frittering away their scholarships on cheap but filling Texan dishes. Live music every evening from 22.30hrs.

El Sid, 322 West 15th Street (between Eighth and Ninth Avenues). A small *tapas* bar with a few excellent main dishes.

Granados, 125 MacDougal Street (tel: 673 5576). Spanish food to live Spanish music.

Hows Bayou Café, 355 Greenwich Street (tel: 925 5405), at the corner of Harrison. For the latest in fashionable cuisines, serving Cajun food from the Southern States. Start with a frozen marguerita before tucking into nachos, gumbo n'awlins (shrimp, sausage, chicken and okra in soup), or bayou chicken (smothered in white gravy with pecans) and either a slice of chocolate or apple pie like nobody's grandma ever made.

Los Panchos, 71 West 71st Street (tel: 874 7336). Good for a weekend Mexican brunch if you find yourself cruising the Upper West Side.

Mary Ann's, 116 Eighth Avenue at 16th Street (tel: 633 0877). Always crowded, always good burritos and enchiladas, and always unmistakably New York. Better to eat here at lunchtime, when there's more space and you can get a bargain, filling meal.

Rosa's Place, 303 West 48th Street between Eighth and Ninth Avenues (tel: 586 4853 or 245 9223). Very fashionable, serving refined Mexican with famous birdbath-size margueritas.

However Fred and Ginger pronounce the name, Grand Central Terminal's Oyster Bar goes down a treat

Southern Funk Café, 330 West 42nd Street at Ninth Avenue in the McGraw-Hill building (tel: 564 6560). There is nothing remotely smart about the place, but good Southern home cooking, like jambalayas, all served cafeteria-style.

Sylvia's Restaurant, 328 Lenox Avenue (tel: 996 0660). The delicious soul food – yams, grits, etc – is one of the best reasons for visiting Harlem.

Tortilla Flats, 767 Washington Street (tel: 243 1053). A funky, inexpensive joint that's jumping in the West Village. It serves fun Tex-Mex dishes to a laid-back crowd. Specialities of the house are Carnitas Colorado and pork burritos with beans and chilli sauce.

Yellow Rose, 450 Amsterdam

FOOD AND DRINK

Avenue (tel: 595 8760). An Upper West Side establishment, good for burgers, ribs and steaks in gigantic Texan proportions.

Rich, Famous or Fashionable

Barbetta, 321 West 46th Street, between Eighth and Ninth Avenues (tel: 246 9171). New York's oldest restaurant (in operation since 1906) has a beautiful Florentine garden which takes this traditional Northern Italian restaurant into the realms of special occasion. The menu is a bit stodgy, but the location in the heart of the theatre district is perfect.

Bouley's, 165 Duane Street (tel: 608 3852). Named after owner-chef David Bouley, this is a relative newcomer on the growing TriBeCa dining circuit. Service and cuisine are excellent – modern and predominantly French, though the cuisine is usually classified as American. Packed with Wall Street yuppies at night, though it is also good for reasonably priced business lunches.

Café Luxembourg, 200 West 70th Street, at Amsterdam and West End (tel: 873 7411). A bohemianesque, French-influenced art deco bistro, serving American food and run by Britisher Brian McNally, of Café Odeon fame in TriBeCa. The bargain is the *prix fixe* early dinner between 17.30 and 18.30hrs, very popular with the pre-Lincoln Center crowds.

Chez Louis, 1016 Second Avenue (tel: 752 1400). Huge portions, strictly for the meat-and-potatoes diner who's planning to start dieting next week. Garlic-flecked potato cake, beef, chicken, duck confit and chocolate cake feature heavily on the menu.

Elaine's, 1703 Second Avenue (tel: 534 8103). Most famous for the opening shot of the film *Manhattan*; now the haunt of well-known authors, TV and movie stars, and the smart, chic set in their Bloomingdale's co-ordinates. The food, however, is unremarkable Italian and very expensive.

Gage and Tollner, 372 Fulton Street (tel: 718 875 5181). One of the best restaurants in Brooklyn and adjacent to the Heights, it reeks of the turn-of-the-century, with white tablecloths, gaslights and reticent waiters serving predominantly seafood dishes.

Ken's Broome St Bar, 363 West Broadway (tel: 925 2086). It used to be a spit-and-sawdust bar, but has followed in the upwardly mobile footsteps of its neighbours. A good place for a moderately priced lunch with a youthful crowd.

Lucy's Retired Surfers Bar and Restaurant, 503 Columbus Avenue at 84th Street (tel: 787 3009). A great seafood restaurant with loud music, which also manages to pack in the drinking crowds around the tiny bar at the front.

O'Neal's Baloon, 48 West 63rd Street (tel: 399 2352). A relaxing burger bar and a good place to meet friends before and after Lincoln Center performances.

The Oyster Bar, Grand Central Terminal, Lower Level (tel: 490 6650). An exception to the station buffet rule, The Oyster Bar in Grand Central Terminal is a grand, tiled and immaculate if somewhat hectic restaurant, packed at lunchtime with office workers. It has a huge range of oysters: Apalachicola, Bluepoint, Chesapeake Bay, Westcott Bay, Malpeque, Chincotengue and many others, plus live Maine lobster and one of the longest white wine lists in America. Closed weekends.

River Café, 1 Water Street (tel: 718 522 5200). In the shadow of Brooklyn Bridge on the Brooklyn side of the river, this barge restaurant serves the best view of the Manhattan skyline, especially romantic at night, when the trees sparkle with fairy lights in the courtyard and on the verandah overlooking the water. The food is good though overpriced, the staff

Looking west over the East River: patrons of the River Café

pretentious. Reservations essential and as far ahead as you can. Boats depart from South Sea Seaport during the summer.

Russian Tea Room, 150 West 57th Street, at 7th Avenue (tel: 265 0947). Next door to Carnegie Deli, this is not a place for tea, but the best restaurant in town for Russian specialities, served in opulent green, red and gold surroundings, often to celebrities and always at high prices. Don't miss their blini with caviar and a glass of chilled vodka.

Saloon Bar and Brasserie, 1920 Broadway at 64th Street (tel: 874 1500). A smart, popular restaurant opposite the Lincoln Center with white tablecloths, black chairs, maroon paintwork and a down-to-earth bar area. Waiters approach you on roller skates bearing huge menus of pasta, salad, burgers, grilled meat and fish specials.

FOOD AND DRINK

Sardi's, 234 West 44th Street (tel: 221 8440). The traditional 'before and after the theatre' restaurant. Stick to the simpler dishes or you will be disappointed.

SoHo Charcuterie, 195 Spring Street at Sullivan (tel: 226 3545). The front is an up-market delicatessen takeaway, while the starkly modern dining room behind serves such refined brunch dishes as truffled pasta, goose livers, and fine cuts of veal.

The Spirit of New York departs from Pier 11 at the end of Wall Street (tel: 279 1890). A luxury cruiser open for lunch, dinner and moonlight cruises around Manhattan.

Spring Street Natural Restaurant, 62 Spring Street at Lafayette Street (tel: 966 0290). Mainly excellent vegetarian dishes, well suited to its artsy surroundings.

Sweet's, 2 Fulton Street, South Street Seaport (tel: 344 9189). The oldest and arguably the best seafood restaurant in New York, dating back to the days of clipper-ships. Fish is fresh from the Fulton Street fish market and superbly cooked, though you will have to keep your elbows in among the crowds.

Umberto's Clam House, 129 Mulberry Street (tel: 431 7545). Most famous for the early '70s murder of gangland leader Joe 'Crazy Joey' Gallo by a rival gang while dining on the excellent seafood.

West End Café, 2911 Broadway (tel: 666 9160). Once a favourite Beat hangout, loved by Ginsberg, Kerouac *et al.* now serves reasonable meals, drinks and live jazz.

Windows on the World, 1 World Trade Center, 107th floor (tel: 938 1111). If you have always wanted to eat with your

You get more than a cuppa in the Russian Tea Rooms; in this opulent setting vodka and caviar have superseded the samovar

eyes feasting on a view of the Manhattan skyline, this is the classic place to do it. The food is broadly Continental and not that exciting but the wine list, with 800 items, is worth tearing your eyes away from your window on the world for at least 10 minutes. Surcharge of $7.50 on weekday lunches.

24-Hour Restaurants

If you get caught with hunger pangs at three in the morning, you will find many delis open especially along Second Avenue. In most neighbourhoods there is at least one 24-hour Korean greengrocer.

Among the all-night stands in New York are:

Around the Clock, 8 Stuyvesant Street and Ninth Avenue (tel: 598 0402)

Empire Diner, 210 10th Avenue at West 22nd Street (tel: 924 0011).

The Green Kitchen, 1477 First Avenue (tel: 988 4163).

Kiev, 117 Second Avenue (tel: 674 4040).

Sarge's Delicatessen and Restaurant, 548 Third Avenue (tel: 679 0442).

103 Second Restaurant, 103 Second Avenue (tel: 533 0769).

Silver Star, 1236 Second Avenue (tel: 249 4250).

West Side Diner, West 31st Street and Ninth Avenue (tel: 560 8407).

Dress

When eating in one of the city's expensive restaurants New Yorkers dress *very* smart. Suits with ties for men, chic outfits and dresses for women, are *de rigueur*. If in doubt ask about the dress code when making a reservation. In less expensive places anything casual goes.

Food Tours

Lou Singer organises 'noshing tours' mostly around the ethnic potpourri of the Lower East Side, where clients sample their way through Benn's farmer cheese stuffed with blueberries, Gus's pickles, Russo's homemade mozzarella, Shapiro's wines and lox with bagels at Russ and Daughters. As Lou, an ex-*New York Times* delivery driver explains, you learn more about the roots of New York in this imaginative way that you would through a hundred more conventional tours. Other, more specialised tours, range from a 'great organ crawl' to 'light and shadows of the wickedest city in the world'. (tel: 718 875 9084 for details).

Opening Times

New Yorkers tend to eat late. You will often find the more expensive places empty and distinctly lacking in atmosphere until at least 20.00hrs. There is rarely a problem getting served at 23.00hrs, even later. Always reserve in the more expensive restaurants, otherwise you run the risk of standing in line or going elsewhere. Some have a 'no reservations' policy, which again can mean a long wait outside, especially for a place recently acclaimed by the foodies.

Those on a budget are likely to find set menus at lunchtime their best bet. Most restaurants are open every evening except Sunday.

SHOPPING

In his movie *Manhattan*, Woody Allen remarks that it would only take the removal of Diane Keaton's Bloomingdale's charge card to force her to reveal secrets of state. To New Yorkers with disposable incomes for such indulgences, shopping is one of the serious compensations for living in the city. If it exists and is for sale, they say, you can buy it in New York.

As with any city, the style of shops can to a large extent be defined by their location. Broadly speaking, if you are after chic exclusivity you will find it in the small clothing boutiques of Madison Avenue on the Upper East Side. If your taste in clothes is more avant garde, then SoHo would make better geographical sense. Trendy gear at budget prices can be found in the Village and good value for little money in the department stores in the midtown area – except of course 'Bloomies' and some of the more elegant stores such as Saks and Lord and Taylor on Fifth Avenue.

Most shops open six days a week and generally open their doors around 10.00hrs, but stay open until 18.00hrs or later, with one late night (around 21.00hrs). Many shops also open on Sundays, from around noon to 17.00hrs. Sunday, but never before midday, is one of the best times for shopping in SoHo, although it does get crowded and some of the best galleries close.

At the weekend you will also stumble across lots of stalls and impromptu markets which are trading on sidewalks and vacant parking lots.

A beacon for discerning shoppers –Bloomingdale's department store

SoHo

The streets of SoHo, with a recent spread into TriBeCa, are the trendy shopping heart of New York, the place for more radical styles in furniture, art, clothes and even household gadgets. Several shops appear more like galleries than the conventional galleries, placing their wares on the same pedestal as works of art. They are certainly as large, often housed in renovated warehouses, converted into wooden-floored showpieces of how the yuppie New Yorker should be dressed and his or her apartment furnished.
Zona, at 97 Greene Street, is one of the most interesting stores. It sells mostly furniture and artefacts from the Southwest, including stained wood farm furniture, Indian rugs and jewellery, terracotta pots, hammered ironware, beeswax candles and sandblasted glass objects.
Umbrello, 379 West Broadway, sells painted, stained 'folk' furniture, with more southwesterly influences.
Ad Hoc Softwares, down the street at number 410, specialises in fancy bathroom accessories, cotton dressing gowns and linens. Several shops under the same roof make up **SoHo Emporium**, at 375 West Broadway, including **Magnifico**, with its 3-D 'sculpted' sweaters.
Dean and DeLuca's, on the corner of Broadway and Prince Street, is guaranteed to inspire anyone to the ways of gastronomy. It recently moved from its mid-SoHo home to the fringes, the first to colonize an area previously devoted to cheap clothes and ladies in curlers. It sells the ultimate ravioli, stuffed with lobster. Among 24 types of sausage, try Tuscanno, made of pork, spices, mozzarella and fresh tomatoes. Their displays are worthy of a gallery. If you cannot afford Dean and DeLuca's, **Balducci's**, in the nearby Village at Sixth Avenue and Ninth Street, is almost as good and just a little less expensive.
La Rue des Rêves, at 139 Spring Street, is a mish mash of everything outrageous, a place where both staff and contents are completely OTT. Malcolm McLaren scratches as you trip over live alsations and Pekinese, wander past trees, a cocktail bar and other oddities on your way to the racks of clothes.
Outback, 382 West Broadway, is for the best of the new breed of Australian clothes designers. Further up at number 386, **D F Sanders and Co** is an unashamedly yuppie paradise, with everything from Filofax refills to home humidifiers. If you prefer to fill a room with one object only, try **Think Big!**, a few doors along, where everything for sale is larger than life, from Kodak slide wall mirrors to safety pins as large as your leg.

Upper West Side

The **Ann Bentley Boutique**, at 379 Amsterdam Avenue, according to the *New York Times* review framed in the window, is 'the kind of store a

Zabar's deli, a kitchen store and culinary Aladdin's Cave

businesswoman heads for', full of smart clothes, while at number 378 is the colourful, designer-owned **Claudia Jane Klein**, featuring what the assistants describe as 'a line of resort clothes'. At number 463 there's **Avventura**, where, according to a *New York Times* shopping guide, 'if Upper West Siders *wanted* to stay home and entertain, this is where they would find the stemware and decanters, the vases and flatware, the candlesticks and bowls to do it in proper yup style'; and **Edith Nostalgia**, at number 469, is full of things that you can remember your parents tossing out into the rubbish bins.

Meanwhile, back in the sweatroom, the **New York Jock** at number 381 is packed with Bermuda shorts and Hawaiian shirts. The changing rooms, incidentally, are tiled and fitted with (non-working) showers. **Banana Republic** specialises in safari styles at several locations, including 87th Street and Broadway, and Bleecker Street and Sixth Avenue. **Hand Block**, on Broadway, has beautifully printed tablecloths and napkins, dishes, vases and other household items. Rummaging through piles of second-hand garments is popular in New York; the difference at **Alice Underground**, 380 Amsterdam Avenue, at the foot of a flight of Victorian steps, is that you can make a beeline for the item you are looking for, as the shop's huge stock of vintage clothes and accessories are beautifully cleaned, pressed and categorized, yet still bargains at the price.

On Broadway at 80th Street you will smell **H&H Bagels**, *the* place for a Sunday morning takeaway bagel. Just up the road on the corner of 80th is **Zabar's**, New York's best kitchen store, including wonderful foods.

Despite its cramped proportions, the **Magazine Store** on Broadway at 62nd Street has periodicals from all over the world. **Maxilla and Mandible**, just along the road from the Museum of Natural History at 451 Columbus, sells bones and is popular with interior decorators, artists and lawyers in need of exhibits for court. A human foot, for example, costs $70, a rat skeleton $12. A notice informs customers that 'all human specimens originally came from medical supply companies'.

Shakespeare and Co, Broadway, between 80th and 81st Streets, is a good bookstore, usually with plenty of opera material. **Paragon Sports**, at 18th and Broadway, has one of the best selections of swimwear in town, including Body Glove, Speedo, Too Hot Brazil and Sasafras. For the budget browser there is a busy market of antiques, jewellery, clothing and kitch every Sunday on Columbus Avenue at 76th.

Upper East Side
The city's most exclusive and chic windows (**Saint Laurent Rive Gauche**, 855 Madison, **Pucci** at 24 East 64th and **Fiorucci** at 125 East 59th), line the avenues and side streets of the Upper East Side, with entry to many accessible only when an assistant buzzes you in. Between them lie a rash of some of the best art galleries and antique shops in town,

particularly along Madison Avenue, between 59th and 79th Streets.

Best antique dealers include **James Robinson** at 12 East 65th Street and **Antique Porcelain Company** at 48 East 57th Street. A nostalgic glimpse of European furniture can be found in shops like **French & Co**, 17 East 65th Street and **Old Versailles** at 152 East 52nd Street. If you want to bid your way into a buy, two of New York's most prestigious auction houses are not far away: **Christie's** at 504 Park Avenue (near 59th Street) and **Sotheby Parke Bernet**, 1334 York Avenue, near 72nd Street.

Midtown
New York's most famous stores – Bergdorf Goodman, Saks, Altman, Tiffany, FAO Schwarz and others – are mostly located along Fifth Avenue (the exception being Macy's on Broadway, Alexander's on Lexington and Bloomingdale's on Third).

Rizzoli is the most attractive of the city's bookstores, though **Dalton's**, at number 666, always seems to carry a much wider stock. The affordable items in **Tiffany's**, at number 727, are on the second floor; best bargains are the silver bookmarks with the Tiffany name. At the other end of the bankruptcy scale the Tiffany Diamond is the world's largest and finest canary diamond, on show on the first floor.

FAO Schwarz, at 767 Fifth Avenue on 58th Street, (tel: 644 9400) the ultimate toy emporium in the US, an extraordinary collection of toys, dolls, stuffed animals and trains from all over the world, now in a new home at the bottom of the General Motors building.

Brooks Brothers, 346 Madison Avenue at 44th Street, have been clothing generations of ivy-league school gentlemen for decades.

Laura Ashley's printed dresses and fabrics are popular, at 714 Madison Avenue.

There are several branches of **The Gap** in town, selling quality jeans, tracksuits and other casual American wear. One of the first to open in New York is at 145 East 42nd Street.

Bigelow Pharmacy, 414 Sixth Avenue, is worth a browse, even if you then buy what you need at the far cheaper **Duane Reed** chain. It's an 1830s chemist, one of the oldest in town with beautiful Victorian fixtures and fittings.

Lower East Side

Though not high on the shopper's itinerary, it is worth detouring to the Lower East Side on a Sunday morning for the **Orchard Street Market** (see page 77). Near by is **Russ and Daughters**, 179 Houston Street, one of the oldest of the district's Jewish foodshops, where the locals queue for smoked and pickled fish, caviar and bagels. The products at **Ben's Cheese Shop**, next-door, are nearly all home-made.

Department Stores

Alexander's, 731 Lexington Avenue at 58th Street (tel: 593 0880) and 4 World Trade Center Plaza (tel: 466 1414); and other branches in Brooklyn, Bronx and Queens. The poor man's answer to Bloomingdale's.

Bergdorf-Goodman, 754 Fifth Avenue (tel: 753 7300). This is where ageing wealthy ladies spend the afternoon caning their charge cards. They could get their accessories cheaper elsewhere but prefer to pay for the elegant atmosphere and sumptuous décor.

Bloomingdale's, 1000 Third Avenue at 60th Street (tel: 705 2000). A more fashionable version of Macy's, 'Bloomies' tends to attract a more discerning and stylish customer. Racks of famous label clothes, a floor of household goods, restaurants and food shops.

Lord and Taylor, 424 Fifth Avenue at 38th Street (tel: 391 3344). Rather stuffy and traditional, but nonetheless the designer classics are reliable in quality.

Macy's, 34th Street and Broadway (tel: 695 4400). The largest store in the world with 'everything for everyone' spread over 10 floors. Fashion, furniture and gadgets for the home, post office, theatre ticket outlet, travel agency, beauty salons and restaurants, including PJ Clarke's basement bar. The food hall is excellent. Also branches in Brooklyn, Queens and Staten Island.

Saks Fifth Avenue, 611 Fifth Avenue at 50th Street at the Rockefeller Center (tel: 753 4000). A landmark for the rich and famous, with eight floors of glitzy designer collections from around the globe.

F W Woolworth: 20 odd branches in Manhattan; one of the largest Woolworth stores in the world is at 120 West 34th Street, just across from Macy's. Stores also at 170 East 42nd Street; 755 Seventh Avenue; and 7–9 Dey Street (opposite the World Trade Center).

Markets

Bargain hunters have to accept that there is no New York equivalent to London's Portobello Road, Paris's Saint-Ouen or Amsterdam's Singels. The closest the city comes is the slightly tacky second-hand clothes and cheap household objects in **Orchard Street** on Sunday, the **Flower District** in West Manhattan on Sixth Avenue (26th to 30th Streets), the Sunday market on **Columbus**, near the Natural History Museum, and the

Sunday best shopping: bargain-hunting in Orchard Street

sporadic neighbourhood block fairs organised by local tenants' associations. The larger markets are always listed in *Village Voice*.

Supermarkets

The main chains, to be found all over town, are **Red Apple**, **Sloan's** and **Grand Union**. They are always open until at least early evening, noisy, hectic and with a wide range of food in large volumes; the cartons of milk and orange juice, for example, are as big as buckets. They also stock chemist goods, takeaway food, often magazines and a comprehensive selection of delicatessen foods.

What to Buy

Exotic kitchenware: upstairs in **Zabar's** on Broadway at 80th Street is devoted to all manner of exciting crockery and kitchen utensils, from Oriental steamers to Italian cappuccino makers, plus American

SHOPPING

gadgets, including can openers that really work. For 'I Love New York' paraphernalia, raid the shops in the west 50s, between Sixth and Eighth Avenues.

Glass objects: intricately hand-painted glass goblets, vases, glasses and other household objects are sold at **Orrefors**, 58 East 57th Street/Park Avenue, though they don't come cheap.

Jeans: the **Canal Jean Co**, 504 Broadway, at Broome and Spring Streets has racks of new and second-hand American Levis, 501s, etc, in a huge, hangar-style warehouse. **The Gap** chain is another good denim bet, as is the **Unique Clothing Warehouse**, 718 Broadway, similar to Canal Jean Co with a design-your-own-T-shirt service.

Jewellery: Diamond row is one of New York's gems, a pocket of opulence along West 47th Street between Fifth and Sixth Avenue that earned its nickname from its shops brimming with wildly expensive gemstones and jewellery.

Music and musical Instruments: **Tower Records** is a music emporium for all kinds of records, cassettes and CDs, including rock, pop, jazz, classical and folk. There are two branches: Broadway at Fourth Street, in the West Village, and Broadway at 67th Street, near the Lincoln Center. For classical music there are several possibilities, including **The Record Hunter**, 507 Fifth Avenue (42nd Street) and **Sam Ash**, at 160 West 48th Street,

one of the most well-known among many shops bulging with musical instruments along 48th Street east of Seventh Avenue for about half a block.

Outdoor gear: everything for the outdoor enthusiast, including rucksacks, hiking boots, mountain jackets, cross country and downhill ski equipment and clothes, cyclewear, tennis, hockey, skating and other sportswear is on sale at **Paragon Sports**, on Broadway at 18th Street. **Hudson's**, at 105 Third Avenue, is another good bet, while **Kreeger**, at 16 West 46th Street, is another favourite with backpackers.

Running clothes: **Super Runners Shop**, 1 Herald Center (Broadway and 33rd Street) and 360 Amsterdam at 77th Street, sells hi-tech shoes and clothing for runners, plus free maps of Central Park running courses. If you want to enter the New York Marathon in October you can apply here.

Silk-screened T-shirts: at the **T-Shirt Gallery of NY**, 154 East 64th Street (corner of Lexington Avenue), they are air-brushed, hand-painted and silk-screened. Custom Corner creates designs in only a few minutes.

Other good shopping areas include Fulton and Water Streets in the South Street Seaport area, A & S Plaza on 33rd Street (Manhattan's largest mall) and the World Trade Center, and several of the museum shops, which stock books, cards, posters and other gift ideas.

*Carlyle Hotel, on the fashionable
Upper East Side*

ACCOMMODATION

There is an abundance of good
hotels to choose from in New
York: more than 100,000
rooms, in fact. However, the
price of real estate in
Manhattan is such that, when
translated into hotel charges
there is no doubt that the roof
over your head will absorb the
bulk of your spending money.
Unlike most European cities,
which contain a large
proportion of central yet
inexpensive *pensions* or bed
and breakfast guesthouses for
the lower budget traveller,
New York's inexpensive
hostelries tend to be seedy, in
high crime locations and
uncomfortable in all senses.
Location is all-important when
picking a place to stay, not only
in the conventional sense of
being close to the sights, but to
avoid those areas where the
streets at night may be dark,
deserted and none too safe to
walk.
What it lacks in modest
accommodation, New York
more than makes up for at the
deluxe end of the market.
Rooms in the best hotels are
superbly equipped, with two-
line telephones, colour TVs
swivelling in the bathroom, fax
plugs, dance-in closets, king-
size beds and cable TV all
rapidly becoming the norm.
You won't get mini bars in
NYC; they are illegal, since you
can check in at 18, but you
have to be 21 to drink. Views
tend to be poor, except in the
very best hotels. Breakfast is
rarely included in the room
rate, although many bedrooms
are equipped with tiny self-
catering sections, called
pantries. You pay for the room,
not per person. There are often
discounts available to families
sharing a room, over
weekends and for long stays.
The most convenient location

ACCOMMODATION

for the visitor is Midtown and the hotels which lie roughly within the square formed by Third Avenue, 40th Street, Seventh Avenue and 60th Street, where double rooms cost anything between $130 and $200 a night. If money is no object, the fashionable and expensive Upper East Side contains a selection of some of the very best of New York's traditional and exclusive hotels, charging anything over $200 a night. At the other end of the pecuniary scale, the leafy Murray Hill area in the East 30s has some quiet, comfortable and more moderately priced establishments. There are also motels near the airports. The New York Convention and Visitors' Bureau publishes a free sheet, *The New York Hotel Guide*. At busy times of year, especially at Christmas, it is advisable to book a room well in advance.

Friday and Saturday nights are bargain time in the grander, predominantly business hotels, with rates reduced by up to 50 per cent as the business expense account customers who flock in during the week return to their own beds. Since rooms can usually be shared by two adults and two children, families get the best deal, and children under 14 can nearly always stay in their parents' room for little or no extra charge. For more comfort at slightly higher prices they should consider junior suites. And if you want to economise by squeezing more adults into the room, most hotels won't object.

One way to find a hotel is through the **Central Reservation Service**, which operates 24 hours a day and covers all hotels in North America. For information and reservations in the New York area, tel: 800 950 0232. When it is time to pay the bill, be prepared for the addition of tax adding an extra cost of up to 20 per cent. If you have made phone calls from your room you will now regret it – surcharges are often extortionate. Throughout your stay you will be expected to tip: the bellboy who carries your bag, the doorman who opens your car door or calls you a taxi and, most demanding of all, the room service waiters.

Hotels
Expensive
Algonquin 59 West 44th Street, 10036 (tel: 840 6800). Shaped by literary traditions – the *New Yorker* is said to have been spawned at its Round Table lunches – and perhaps best known as a beautiful setting for afternoon tea. It has recently spent $12 million restoring its original Edwardian décor (just in time, as some of the rooms were getting decidedly shabby), adding such 20th-century touches as air-conditioning and fax plugs. Run by a British manager, Edward Pitt, it has 165 rooms, small by New York standards.
Carlyle 35 East 76th Street at Madison Avenue, 10021 (tel: 744 1600). What New York lacks in the way of European

ambience, it more than makes up for in this sumptuous hotel, a few minutes' walk from the Whitney Museum on the Upper East Side. Its 500 rooms are larger than average, with every whim catered for, including jam-packed refrigerators. You can even get your dog walked. Afternoon tea in the Café Carlyle, listening to jazz or Bobby Short on the piano, is the New World's favourite 'society' pastime.

Grand Bay 152 West 51st Street, Equitable Center, 10019 (tel: 765 1900). The old Taft hotel re-opened in August 1987 as an elegant town house style, and the only luxury hotel on the West Side. 178 quiet rooms with terrible views, but well compensated by the plush furnishings and the 250 film video library.

Marriott Marquis 1535 Broadway at 45/46th Streets, 10036 (tel: 398 1900). A 'city within a city' and one of New York's newest hotels. It claims to have the world's largest indoor atrium, half as tall as the Empire State Building (the reception desk is on the eighth floor). There is a health club, an entire level devoted to shops, a revolving restaurant and 1,871 bedrooms. The Marquis was the first of the smart hotels to be built on Times Square, once considered to be the kiss of death.

Mayfair Hotel Baglioni 610 Park Avenue at 65th Street, 10021 (tel: 288 0800). Two hundred rooms, mostly suites, but only 150 are 'transient' as

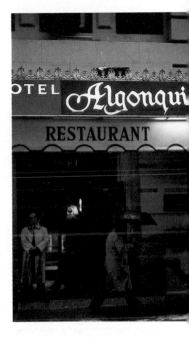

Reputedly the birthplace of the **New Yorker,** *the Algonquin Hotel offers Edwardian luxury*

opposed to residential. A member of Leading Hotels of the World, located on the smart Upper East Side, New York's Mayfair has plenty of airs and graces. Le Cirque restaurant and the pretty, sunken lobby for afternoon tea are very popular. One of New York's Baby Grands, which include the Carlyle, the Pierre and the Ritz-Carlton.

Morgans 237 Madison Avenue at 37/38th Streets, 10016 (tel: 686 0300). Partners Steve Rubell and Ian Schrager have created a hotel that tries not to seem like one, and certainly

A star of the silver screen: the Plaza Hotel looks over Central Park

doesn't even call itself one. 'We are a new concept in nightlife and entertainment in Manhattan', maintains Rubell, of Studio 54 and Palladium fame. French designer Andrée Putnam created an unconventional environment that, in her own phrase, 'would cater to a vertical market based on lifestyle and attitude rather than financial consideration'. With stereo cassettes in every room and VCRs available for loan, displays of Robert Mapplethorpe photographs, bathrooms tiled in black and white hi-tech geometric patterns with stainless steel sinks and hospital fixtures, and a hotel staff clad in Calvin Klein and Giorgio Armani designed uniforms, Morgans is geared to

stay-up-late fashion designers and such superstars as Mick Jagger, Cher and Boy George; *not* the briefcase-encumbered businessman,
Le Parker Meridien 118 West 57th Street at Sixth Avenue (main entrance on 56th), 10019 (tel: 245 5000). A *tranche* of France in Manhattan, with an atmosphere so French you almost expect a fug of Gauloises to meet your nostrils as you enter the lobby. On the contrary, however, Air France's hotel is airy, light and modern. It also has one of the best fitness centres in town, complete with jogging track, high-rise pool and sunbathing deck; and the

excellent Maurice restaurant (French, of course).

The Peninsula New York 700 Fifth Avenue at 55th Street, 10019 (tel: 247 2200). A luxurious art nouveau establishment on the site of the celebrated Maxim's, which opened in 1988 on the site of the landmark Gotham Hotel. 250 luxury rooms, the epitome of lingering Parisian elegance, the majority of which are suites with king-size marble bathrooms. A few even have whirlpool baths. The restaurant Adrienne and less formal Bistro d'Adrienne are also French, while French pastries and afternoon tea are served in the Gotham Lounge. There is also a tri-level, glass enclosed rooftop health spa, with spectacular views.

Plaza 768 Fifth Avenue at 59th Street, Central Park South, 10019 (tel: 759 3000). The grand old dame of New York's top hotels, a tall, French château of a building built in 1907 and now an official National Historic Landmark. It is as famous for tea in the Palm Court and drinks at the Oak Bar as for the 812 rooms. The hotel was recently bought by Donald Trump and has been undergoing renovations, but it will still look familiar to those who have seen *Breakfast at Tiffany's, Barefoot In The Park, The Way We Were* and *Plaza Suite.* You will pay most for a room with a view of Central Park; the most famous is the Plaza Suite.

Plaza Athenée 37 East 64th Street, 10021 (tel: 734 9100). A small, luxury Trusthouse Forte hotel, with a noticeably Continental décor of tapestries, antiques, hand-woven carpets and Italian marble. Every room has a gilt clock, fresh flowers, trouser press and towelling robes in the bathroom.

Ritz-Carlton 112 Central Park South at 59th Street, 10019 (tel: 757 1900). The walls are hung with cool, heavy oil paintings depicting British scenes that have become the group's hallmark, even in desert climes. Ask for a room at the front for stunning views over Central Park, though a bed at the back is considerably cheaper. Nancy Reagan ranks among its more famous fans.

Waldorf-Astoria 301 Park Avenue at 49/50th Streets, 10022 (tel: 355 3000). A prestigious Park Avenue address – 'meet me at the Waldorf' has long echoed around the upper echelons of society – the Waldorf is worth a visit just to see the art deco lobby with its giant clock. It was built for the Chicago World Fair in 1893 and lovingly transported from the original hotel, now razed to the ground to make way for the Empire State Building.

Medium-priced

Hotel Beverly 125 East 50th Street at Lexington Avenue, 10022 (tel: 753 2700). Value for money with comfortable, unpretentious rooms. Suites with kitchen facilities are a perfect choice for families; others have terraces, a luxury in space-conscious Manhattan. There is also a restaurant, coffee shop and pharmacy.

Chelsea 222 West 23rd Street, 10011 (tel: 243 3700). Chelsea

ACCOMMODATION

was the home of the theatre district in the 19th century, and the Chelsea Hotel has traditionally been the place for bohemians to hang out. Mark Twain and Tennessee Williams loved it so much they lived here. Other famous hangers-on include Dylan Thomas, Bob Dylan and Jack Kerouac. The décor is beautifully Edwardian, at the shabby edges.

Doral Court 130 East 39th Street at Lexington Avenue, 10016 (tel: 685 1100). Newly re-vamped and now better than its two related neighbours, **Doral Park Avenue** (70 Park Avenue, tel: 687 7050) and big brother **Doral Inn** (541 Lexington Avenue, tel: 755 1200). Everything the budget-minded traveller could want: clean, comfortable rooms, huge beds and a fridge. Dinner is served in the Courtyard Café.

Hotel Elysée 60 East 54th Street, 10022 (tel: 753 1066). One of New York's more unusual hotels, a far cry from the could-be-anywhere chain. Each room has its own name and décor.

Good meals are served in the Pisces restaurant, where you can eat while letting your eyes scan the impressive ceiling to floor mural of the French Riviera.

Gramercy Park 2 Lexington Avenue at 21st Street, 10010 (tel: 475 4320). A favourite with visitors from Europe, possibly because its size is manageable and it is situated in a peaceful residential district; perhaps because they have access to the private park, two minutes' walk away.

Mayflower Hotel on the Park 15 Central Park West at 61st Street, 10023 (tel: 265 0060). An excellent position on Central Park, yet slightly cheaper than the other ageing beauty hotels near by, since it's getting slightly down at heel. The guests, predominantly artsy, tend to hang out in the Conservatory Café.

Royalton 44 West 44th Street (tel: 869 4400). Earned its reputation mainly by being the cheap place across the street from the Algonquin: drink in one, pay for a room in the other.

St Moritz on-the-Park 50 Central Park South at Sixth Avenue 10019 (tel: 755 5800). A characterful place to stay, long hailed as the 'Biggest Little Hotel' in New York. But it is perhaps as famous for its sidewalk café, the ice cream it serves in Rumplemayer restaurant and Harry's Bar, as for its 679 rooms.

Salisbury 123 West 57th Street, 10019 (tel: 246 1300). A good value place to stay. Centrally located, opposite the Russian Tea Room, you can book a suite which sleeps four and includes a kitchenette for self-catering. Or there's the pleasant, inexpensive Terrace Café downstairs.

Wales 1295 Madison Avenue, between 92nd and 93rd Streets, 10128 (tel: 876 6000). Causing quite a stir on the Upper East Side, the Wales has had a complete facelift. The end product will be superb. The restaurant, Sarabeth's, is a favourite brunch spot.

Wyndham 42 West 58th Street, 10019 (tel: 753 3500). With a

A limo stretches outside the Wyndham Hotel, showbiz favourite

reputation established by the late Sir Laurence Olivier, the Wyndham has long been a favourite with visiting showbiz personalities from the US and the UK. It has 200 delightful rooms, highly individual, unmodernised and far less expensive than they could be. In fact, you would never know New York was on the outside. The finishing homely touch is the bell you ring for entry.

Inexpensive
Excelsior 45 West 81st Street, 10024 (tel: 362 9200). In a pleasant area near Central Park and the Natural History Museum, only a quick subway or cab ride from downtown.
The Gorham New York 136 West 55th Street, 10019 (tel: 245 1800). Lovely large rooms in modern Italian style, very reasonably priced and all with self-catering facilities.
Howard Johnson Plaza 851 Eighth Avenue, at 51st Street,

10019 (tel: 581 4100). This is one of a chain of three midtown motels, as comfortable but characterless as their type always is, but with good car parking facilities and close to midtown attractions.
Pickwick Arms 230 East 51st Street, 10023 (tel: 355 0300). A good, basic hotel, which is particularly popular with tourists.
Radisson Empire 44 West 63rd Street, 10023 (tel: 265 7400). Conveniently near the Lincoln Center. Pre- and post-concert refreshments are popular at O'Neal's Balloon Café, which is situated opposite the Center.
Washington Square 103 Waverly Place, 10011 (tel: 777 9515). One of the few inexpensive downtown hotels, with an excellent Greenwich Village location. Basic but clean.

YMCAs and Youth Hostels
Amandla House Hostel 722 St Nicholas Avenue at 146th Street (tel: 926 7030). Only open to overseas visitors. Maximum stay allowed is limited to five days.

ACCOMMODATION

There are four YMCAs (known as Ys) in town which are mixed sex. All are clean, safe, well-positioned and have good facilities. Vanderbilt and West Side even have swimming pools. Book well in advance, as they are often block-booked.
McBurney YMCA 206 West 24th Street, 10011 (tel: 741 9226).
Vanderbilt YMCA 224 East 47th Street at Second Avenue, 10017 (tel: 755 2410).
West Side YMCA 5 West 63rd Street, 10023 (tel: 787 4400).
American Youth Hostels (AYH) Upper West Side at 891 Amsterdam Avenue, West 103rd Street, 10025 (tel: 932 2300). Has its largest hostel in New York, a century-old city block only recently converted. A stay is limited to seven days. *Subway*: 103rd Street.

Bed and Breakfast

In America, particularly New York, B&B is a relatively new alternative to hotels. The accommodation's main appeal to visitors lies in its high standard of homeliness, an environment shaped by the personality – and often prosperity – of the hosts. For the first time visitor, B&B is a less awesome alternative to towering, impersonal skyscrapers.

The typical hosts are often professionals whose children have grown up and left, leaving them echoing around a too-large house. Rather than sell it or let the spare rooms to permanent lodgers, they indulge their interest in meeting overseas travellers by opening their doors to visitors. In a lot of

properties there are three or four bedrooms and you can expect a telephone, TV and radio in the room and a bathroom *en suite*. Several have jacuzzis or swimming pools. It is not unusual for your host to lend you a bicycle, arrange theatre tickets and steer you towards the best local sights, events and restaurants. You will probably have a key to the front door and can come and go as you please.

When travelling around you're unlikely to see B&B signs outside houses, so to be sure of a room, contact hosts or agencies well in advance, at least a month ahead.

Agencies in the US who can be contacted direct for listings of B&Bs:

Bed and Breakfast

Abode Bed and Breakfast, PO Box 20022, NY 10028 (tel: 472 2000).
At Home in New York, PO Box 407, New York NY 10185 (tel: 956 3125 or 265 8539).
Bed and Breakfast Network of New York, 134 West 32nd Street, NY 10001 (tel: 645 8134).
City Lights, PO Box 20355, Cherokee Station, NY 10028 (tel: 737 7049).
New World Bed & Breakfast 150 Fifth Avenue, Suite 711, NY 10011 (tel: 675 5600).
New Yorkers at Home 301E 60th Street, NY 10022 (tel: 838 7015).
Urban Ventures PO Box 426, Planetarium Station, NY 10024 (tel: 594 5650). The first such agency to have set up in New York, and still arguably the best of all the B&B agencies available.

NIGHTLIFE AND ENTERTAINMENT

Entertainmentwise, as they say, the city simmers away from dawn till dawn, deeming the TV virtually redundant. The chances are that anything you want to do will be on tap somewhere in Manhattan. For the theatre buff this not only means Broadway but also Off and Off Off Broadway – which refers not only to the position of the theatres but the types of production you are likely to see. Musical performances are equally varied, spanning Opera at the Met (Metropolitan Opera House), concert and ballet at Carnegie Hall, jazz at the Village Gate and heavy metal rock concerts at Madison Square Garden.

Enjoying a drink in Fanelli's. The wood-panelled bar is popular with the Wall Street set

What's On Listings

The best sources of entertainment are the *Village Voice* (particularly for events in Greenwich Village and SoHo), published weekly, and *New York Magazine*, also weekly. The thick Sunday edition of the *New York Times* is comprehensive for mainstream events, while its *Weekend* section on Friday lists ticket availability. The New York Convention and Visitors Bureau publishes an Official Broadway Theatre and City Guide (free).

Ballet

There are five major ballet companies in New York: **Alvin Ailey** Offbeat ballet and modern jazz performances, heavily influenced by traditional ethnic oppression. They perform most regularly at City Center Theater, 131 West 55th Street (tel: 581 7907).

American Ballet Theater A huge, traditional ballet company (mainly 19th-century and early 20th-century classics) which performs from mid April to mid June at the Metropolitan Opera House in the Lincoln Center (tel: 362 6000).
Eliot Feld Ballet Joyce Theater, 175 Eighth Avenue (tel: 242 8000).
Joffrey Ballet 131 West 55th Street (tel: 265 7300). One of five resident dance troupes at the City Center Theater. It performs its fair share of 20th-century classics but is renowned for ultra-hip contemporary works and flits between New York and Los Angeles.
New York City Ballet Over a hundred dancers make this the largest (and arguably the best) dance company in the West. The main choreographers are the Russian emigré Balanchine and Jerome Robbins. The company spends six months of the year at the New York State Theater in the Lincoln Center

Everything but the movies: the Odeon bar has a cosmopolitan air

Plaza (tel: 870 5570). If you are in town over the Christmas period, don't miss Balanchine's traditional December production of *The Nutcracker.*

Bars
In New York you don't just go to a bar. You go to a bar to eat, meet a friend, catch some jazz, pick up a partner, bop the night away, take away a burger or listen to a cabaret act. You need to do a little homework before picking your bar. If you are a couple, for example, you would be bored by the singles and predominantly male Irish bars along Second and Third Avenues, between 50th and 70th Streets; and by the bulk of the gay bars around the Village (among the better known are **Marie's Crisis Café** at 59 Grove Street, **The Monster** on Sheridan Square and **TY's** on Christopher Street).

However, in recent years, Aids has played havoc with the singles scene. Heavy leather bars on the West Side (Badlands, Ramrod, Anvil, etc) have either closed or wound down, while many singles heterosexual bars are giving way to pool halls such as **Spo-Dee-O-Dees** on West 73rd Street. (See also **Personal Priorities**, page 101.)

Most bars open around lunchtime and have closed by 04.00hrs; minimum drinking age is strictly 21 years. The following is a very select list. For further listings, see **Food and Drink**, page 56, and the **Music** section, page 91.

Canal Bar 511 Greenwich Street/Spring Street (tel: 334 5150). A restaurant-cum-bar, currently so much in vogue that reservations are absolutely essential after 22.00hrs.

Fanelli's 94 Prince Street (tel: 226 9412). One of the city's most historic bars encrusted in dark wood, now a favourite with the monied Wall Street yuppies.

Oak Bar Fifth Avenue/Central Park South (tel: 759 3000). In the Plaza Hotel. This is a favourite establishment with the loaded (in the bank balance sense).

Odeon 145 West Broadway/Thomas Street (tel: 233 0507). A converted '50s cafeteria, with all its original art deco trimmings retained, which feels more like somewhere in Paris, especially at the bar, which runs the length of one wall. Even the paddle fans above the restaurant tables seem to turn to the rhythm of the Big Band piped music.

Pete's Tavern 129 East 18th Street (tel: 473 7676). Recommended to anyone who wants to sample a taste of old New York.

PJ Clarke's 915 Third Avenue/55th Street (tel: 759 1650). The preppies' hangout, very male and den-like. Good burgers.

Rusty's 1271 Third Avenue/73rd Street (tel: 861 4518). Very sporty; haunt of the Mets and other personalities. It also happens to have a gigantic TV screen.

Cabaret

New York excels in good comedy and cabaret, from amateurs wandering on stage for their first taste of the microphone to top names, billed for weeks beforehand and charging exorbitant prices. Nightly shows are the norm at most clubs, often two at weekends (the first at about 21.00hrs, another around midnight). Full listings are available in *New York Magazine*.

The big revival in New York nightlife is cabaret supperclubs and dinner dancing, both available in the **Rainbow Room**, 30 Rockefeller Plaza, in the Rockefeller Center (tel: 632 5100). Recently restored to its glamorous Fred Astaire and Ginger Rogers heyday style (the midst of the Great Depression), the Rainbow Room re-opened at the time of the October crash. The music is '30s and Latin: the two bands change throughout the evening, but it's difficult to see the seam. Very popular with New York yuppies, with six weeks' advance booking for weekends, otherwise two weeks. Tickets include an excellent dinner.

Other venues include:
The Ballroom 253 West 28th/Eighth Avenue (tel: 244 3005). Comedy, singers plus *tapas* and drinks.
Café Carlyle Madison Avenue/76th Street (tel: 570 7189). The most regular performer is singer Bobby Short.
Café Versailles 151 East 50th Street (tel: 753 3429). New York's answer to the Parisian revue, complete with can-can-style chorus line and feathered plumes.
Caroline's Comedy Club 1626 Broadway (tel: 757 4100). Comedy clubs have been flourishing ever since the TV satirical *Saturday Night Live*, made in New York, became a cult in the '70s.
Catch A Rising Star 1487 First Avenue/78th Street (tel: 794 1906). You have the chance to catch one any night of the week.
Comedy U 55 Grand Street (tel: 431 4022). On Wednesday night the unknowns get a chance to raise a laugh; on Thursday performers are women-only; Friday to Sunday are stand-up comics and ad libbers (two performances on Friday, three on Saturday).
Comic Strip Inc. 1568 Second Avenue/82nd Street (tel: 861 9386). Famous for its stand-up comics and aspiring singers. Open every night from 21.00hrs.

Dangerfield's 1118 First Avenue, between 61st and 62nd Streets (tel: 593 1650). One of the oldest comedy clubs in the city, brainchild of comedian Rodney Dangerfield two decades ago, and still having them rolling in the aisles.
Duplex 61 Christopher Street (tel: 255 5438). Another favourite with good, as-yet-unknown comedians and entertainers, one of the most popular in the Village, particularly amongst the gay community. Two shows every night. Or you may prefer to

Cabaret is available in all shapes and forms. The Café Carlyle, in the exclusive Carlyle Hotel, is one of the city's cabaret venues

visit the raucous piano bar downstairs.
Jan Wallman's 49 West 44th/Fifth Avenue (tel: 764 8930). Recently moved to midtown from the Village, able to draw top artists.

Cinema

The movie scene flourishes in New York, and you will always find screenings of the latest releases. Films are often staged throughout the day, with programmes starting on alternate hours. Offbeat, black and white, alternative, cult or budget films are rather more difficult to unearth; the best place for listings is the *Village Voice*. New Yorkers treat the cinema (or 'movie theater', as it is known here) with reverence: dinner party talk revolves around it, the papers carry listings daily, cinemas have many screenings per day and you will almost always have to queue for a new release.

New York's answer to Cannes is the New York Film Festival, produced by the Film Society of Lincoln Center and held for around two weeks from the end of September. Most performances are held at Alice Tully Hall, though the opening and closing nights are always at Avery Fisher Hall. The cinemas on the East Side are the most expensive; for example, the **Beekman**, Second Avenue at 66th Street and **Coronet**, Second Avenue at 59th Street.

For old foreign and American classics, try **La Guardia** in the Village; **Cinema Village**, 100 3rd Avenue; and **Theatre 80**, St Marks Place, Eighth Street and Second Avenue.

Music

Writing about the flourishing rock club scene in an issue of the *New York Times* magazine, Susan Shapiro claimed that 'all of them aim for the same effect: to blast our perspective beyond the dull comfort of the mainstream. Techno rock, nerd rock, porno rock, nuevo wavo – there's something for every taste, and lots for those with no taste.' But America's music scene has remained rather stultified in recent years: street sounds still tend to be rap and hip hop, and reggae throbs away in Brooklyn and Queens, far from tourist haunts. Many of New York's youth have a nostalgic hankering for the '50s and '60s; they are as likely to be tuned in to Led Zeppelin as to Belinda Carlisle.

Concerts/Opera

Lovers of classical music will find plenty of choice in New York. Expect to queue, especially for the free New York Philharmonic performances in Central Park. Half price tickets, available on the day, are sold at the **Music and Dance Booth** in Bryant Park, 42nd Street, East of Sixth Avenue (tel: 382 2323) (open Tuesday, Thursday and Friday, noon-14.00hrs; 15.00-19.00hrs; Wednesday and Saturday 11.00-14.00hrs, and 15.00-19.00hrs; Sunday noon-18.00hrs). Monday concert tickets are available on the Sunday before the performance.

NIGHTLIFE

Venues include:

Brooklyn Academy of Music
30 Lafayette Avenue, Brooklyn
(tel: 718 636 4126). 'BAM' is
the oldest performing arts
academy in New York, as
famous for its avant garde
dance productions as for its
musical extravaganzas. Visitors
in spring should try to get
tickets for the Festival of Black
Dance, the best of New York's
ethnic girations.
Carnegie Hall 154 West 57th
Street (tel: 247 7800). Probably
the best known venue in the
country for regular classical
and a variety of other
concerts.
Lincoln Center The city's most
famous complex for leading
orchestras and virtuosos,
which tends to feature the
world's best and most
expensive. The **Metropolitan
Opera Company** (the 'Met'),
for example, is located here,
performing from September to
mid April (tel: 362 6000) –
during the summer it vacates
its home for the American
Ballet Theater. Within the
Center there are also the
smaller and cheaper **New
York City Opera** in the New
York State Theater (tel: 870
5570) and the **New York
Philharmonic Orchestra**,
based permanently in Avery
Fisher Hall (tel: 875 5700).
Chamber orchestras and string
quartets perform regularly in
Alice Tully Hall (tel: 875 5000).
During the summer there are
free concerts in Central Park
and free jazz and chamber
music concerts held on the
Music Barge in Brooklyn

Heights at the far end of
Brooklyn Bridge: further details
from **Bargemusic**, Fulton Ferry
Landing, Brooklyn (tel: 718 624
4061).

Jazz
Jazz, unlike rock, has a strong
following in NYC, particularly
in the clubs and bars of
Greenwich Village. The choice
of venues is huge:
Blue Note, 131 West Third
Street at MacDougal Street (tel:
475 8592). Once inside the
place feels like a noisy
aquarium. You pay for the
famous names but plenty are
willing to shell out. If you can
wait until 02.00hrs, however,
you will often walk into free jam
sessions.
Fat Tuesday's, 190 Third
Avenue at 17th Street (tel: 533
7902). For more traditional
jazz, head downstairs to this
club's mirrored basement, the
mecca of jazz to many city fans,
where big stars perform every
evening.
Fifty Five, 55 Christopher
Street (tel: 929 9883). A good
place for jazz, both on the
jukebox and live.
Greene Street Café, 101
Greene Street/Princes Street
(tel: 925 2415). It is possible to
listen from the bar but you
won't see very much – better
to pay for a balcony seat or go
the whole way and book a
table for a meal.
Michael's Pub, 211 East 55th
Street (tel: 758 2272). Woody
Allen has been known to play
clarinet here on certain
Monday nights – but you have
to pay for a meal, and the
atmosphere and prices are

New York is a mecca for lovers of music, with some of the world's top venues and companies

those of a plush restaurant rather than a spit-and-sawdust jazz club.

Sweet Basil, 88 Seventh Avenue/Bleecker Street (tel: 242 1785). By far the most popular jazz restaurant in town. Join the crowds hanging out over long Saturday and Sunday brunches, taking advantage of free music all afternoon.

Village Vanguard, 178 Seventh Avenue South/11th Street (tel: 255 4037). The oldest jazz venue in the city, which is still pulling in the top musicians. To enjoy it you must appreciate crowds.

Other good places include:

Angry Squire, 216 Seventh Avenue (tel: 242 9066).
Bradley's, 70 University Place and 10th Street (tel: 228 6440) and **Small's Paradise**. 2294

Seventh Avenue in Harlem (tel: 234 6330).

Nightclubs/Discos
Within Manhattan's crowded boundaries, you will find some of the most glamorous and lavishly decorated palaces for having a good time in the world.

They are not, however, easy places for the visitor. Not only do they close as fast as they open, but the most popular places can be impossible to get into. You have to queue for ages and, at the door, be scrutinised by arrogant doormen, the censoring equivalent of the Parisian concierge crone – though the former have a definite preference for women and bizarre dressers. It's not unknown for a woman to be 'accepted' and her partner refused. Entry prices may or may not include a first drink. Current 'hot' places to dance the night away include:

Copacabana, 10 East 60th/Fifth.

Avenue (tel: 755 6010). More famous in its former life as a cabaret/supper club in which every top singer appeared. It closed down in 1973 and re-opened three years later as a disco featuring live bands.

Johnny Rock-It, 901 Broadway at 20th Street (tel: 533 1887). This glassy, glossy bar/disco/restaurant attracts tanned guys who drink Bud and girls who sip pastel-coloured frozen cocktails. The restaurant is informal with burgers and pastas; there's also a disco downstairs.

The Limelight, 47 West 20th Street/Sixth Avenue (tel: 807 7850). This place caused a buzz in 1984 when it took over the landmark gothic Church of the Holy Communion. It has a superb disco but, like the Tunnel (below), is already beginning to be labelled as *passé*.

MK, 204 Fifth Avenue (tel: 779 1340). A sitting room atmosphere like Nell's (below), but lighter décor with marbled walls and stuffed Dobermans. Until 1988 the building was a bank (the cloakroom used to be the safe) and you will only feel at home here if you are young, wealthy and beautifully chic.

Nell's, 246 West 14th Street/Eighth Avenue (tel: 675 1567). An overgrown Edwardian drawing room. 'Guests' lounge on red velvet sofas on the ground floor, sipping exotic cocktails from the bar and wander downstairs every so often to the dance floor.

Palladium, 126 East 14th Street/Third Avenue (tel: 473 7171). Housed in a huge old theatre, with excellent acoustics and lighting: perfect for a hard night's dancing.

You'd better make sure you are not operating on a tight budget when considering Michael's pub, where prices are up-market

Roseland, 239 West 52nd Street/Broadway (tel: 249 8870). Definitely not a disco, but an old-fashioned ballroom. However, late on Friday and Saturday nights there is a concession to pop enthusiasts.

SOB's, 204 Varick Street at West Houston (tel: 243 4949). Its name stands for Sounds of Brazil, not the usual American curse. Latin sounds and a good bar.

Stringfellows, 35 East 21st Street (tel: 254 2444). Transforms every night (except Sundays) at 23.00hrs from a restaurant into an elegant dance club.

Trixie's, 307 West 47th Street (tel: 582 5480). Every New York nightclub seems to have a former life and Trixie's is no exception, its ghosts being Greek waiters serving retsina and olives. You have to eat here, and there is little room to dance to the honeyed voices that stroll up and down between the tables. However everyone seems to love singing along to the loud rock that blasts out of the speakers between live performances.

The Tunnel, 220 12th Avenue/27th Street (tel: 244 6444). As the name suggests, its acoustics reverberate around a converted railway tunnel – even the old tracks are part of the décor, the object of fickle laser lights. The disco is excellent and the dance floor gets extremely crowded.

The World, 254 East Second Street. Also stages regular rock'n'roll concerts when it's not reaping the benefits as an incredibly popular dance club.

Other popular night spots include:

The Cat Club, 76 East 13th Street (tel: 505 0090).
Kingfisher Room, 67 Bleecker Street (tel: 529 1477).
Private Eye's, 40 West 21st Street (tel: 206 7770).
Reggae Lounge, 285 West Broadway (tel: 226 4598).
The Saint, 233 East Sixth Street (tel: 477 0866).

Rock

There are pitifully few places to hear good live rock or blues music in New York. Big name bands, many imported from Britain, play at Madison Square Garden; otherwise you have to rely on neighbourhood bars, particularly in the East Village and Lower East Side, where the music usually emanates from a loud jukebox rather than a stage. Best rock bars include:

Be-Bop Café, 28 West Eighth Street (tel: 982 0802). The drinks are a bit pricey, but the burgers and pasta dishes are good value. The speakers emit loud and raunchy music.

The Bottom Line, 15 West Fourth Street at Broadway (tel: 228 6300). Draws a predominantly student crowd from nearby NY University. The selection ranges from rock or rhythm and blues to jazz.

CBGB, 315 Bowery/Bleecker Street (tel: 982 4052). Birthplace of American punk. The letters stand for country, blue grass and blues but that's the last thing you will hear.

Folk City, 130 West Third Street (tel: 254 8449). Every so often big name folk artists

Broadway is bright and brash and seldom self-effacing. Ticket prices reflect its self-confidence

appear here; the rest of the time, it's an amiable, laid-back venue for leftover hippy music and drinks. At weekends Folk City also stages good value improvised comedy sessions.
Puffy's, 81 Hudson Street (tel: 766 9159). Down by the river in TriBeCa and not yet on the tourist circuit, yet loved by its regulars who come for cheap lunches and drink and a throbbing jukebox.
Village Gate, Bleecker and Thomson Streets (tel: 475 5120). An enormous space with

both rock and jazz on the billings as well as salsa.

Theatre
Just to the north of Times Square is the Great White Way, the part of Broadway synonymous with the theatre. If you know the London stage, you are unlikely to find the New York offering, musicals apart, worthy of applause, especially with ticket prices being that much higher. However, if you want to catch *Phantom of the Opera, Les Misérables, Aspects of Love, Cats* or any other big Broadway hit, it is advisable to write for tickets as far in advance as possible.

A compromise would be to soak up the Broadway atmosphere in Sardi's restaurant at 234 West 44th Street, and enjoy some of New York's experimental theatre productions, 'Off' and 'Off Off' Broadway, which are among the very best in the world. Staged in anything from a one-bulb garage to a converted church, there is an enormous range of productions.

The terms 'Off' and 'Off Off' refer essentially to ticket price, the amount the actors are paid, and the size of the theatre. Comb the pages of the *New York Times* (especially on Sundays) and the *Village Voice* for listings. For information on 'Off Off' productions call: Ticket Central 279 4200.

Half Price Tickets

It is always worth trying to get hold of the half price tickets for

A London musical gets the New York treatment

Broadway and Off Broadway shows, sold on the day of performance at three TKTS booths.

The main one is in Times Square, selling tickets after 10.00hrs for that day's matinées and after 15.00hrs for evening performances. Matinée and Sunday tickets can be purchased the day before the performance, as well as tickets from same-day evening performances, from the TKTS booth at 2 World Trade Center (mezzanine level), Lower Manhattan; and the booth on Court and Montague Streets, Brooklyn. The latter two open Monday to Friday (Brooklyn, Tuesday to Friday), 11.00-17.30hrs; Saturday 11.00-15.30hrs. The earlier you can start queuing, the better. Only cash or travellers' cheques are accepted.

Theatre District Restaurants

Best places to sit and eat while plucking up courage to ask a

NIGHTLIFE

star for an autograph are:
Barrymore's, 267 West 45th Street.
Café Madeleine, 43rd and Ninth Avenue.
Charlie's Restaurant, 705 Eighth Avenue.
Orso, 322 West 46th Street.

Theatre Tours

Backstage on Broadway, 228 West 47th Street (tel: 575 8065). Provides the opportunity to learn about the famous theatre district from professional stage managers, actors, directors or designers on a conducted tour that shows just how a show is put together 'from concept to closing'.
Tours depart daily at 10.30hrs Monday to Saturday, and last up to one and a half hours. Popular Off and Off Off Broadway venues and theatre companies:
Circle Repertory Theater, 99 Seventh Avenue on Sheridan Square (tel: 924 7100). Centrally based in Greenwich Village and a good place for up and coming plays.
La Mama Experimental Theater Company, 74A East Fourth Street (tel: 254 6468). A huge range of avant garde theatrical performances.
New York Shakespeare Festival, Catch Joseph Papp's latest production in the Delacorte Theater in Central Park. Shows are free and held from June to September. Tickets are distributed, one per person, on a first-come, first-served basis Tuesday to Sunday beginning at 18.15hrs. For details you can phone

locally: 861-PAPP.
Public Theater, 425 Lafayette Street at 8th Street/Astor Place (tel: 598 7150). The best place to catch both new and old favourite productions by Joseph Papp, who founded the New York Shakespeare Festival and produced *A Chorus Line* and *Pirates of Penzance*.
Sullivan Street Playhouse, at 181 Sullivan Street, Greenwich Village (tel: 674 3838). The Fantasticks have been playing their whimsical musical here for around 20 years.
The Village Gate Bleecker Street/Thomson Street (tel: 475 5120). A popular place for offbeat jazz, plays and comedy.
Westside Arts Center 407 West 43rd Street (tel: 307 4100). So small the audience is almost taking part.

Twofers

These are genuine 'two tickets for the price of one' slips, available for certain shows that aren't doing too well, which touts offer to the waiting TKTS queues, though they are also widely available in shops, hotels and the Department of Cultural Affairs at 2 Columbus Circle, 59th Street and Broadway. Having bought one of these you can then take it straight to the relevant theatre box office.

Reputable theatre ticket agencies:
Golden and LeBlang, 1501 Broadway (tel: 944 8910).
Hickey's, 251 West 45th Street (tel: 586 2980).

WEATHER AND WHEN TO GO

The best months for sightseeing in New York are May, June, September and October. As any native will tell you, summer in the city takes on a new meaning after a week in a New York heatwave. July and August temperatures frequently hit the high 80s°F (30s°C) and can top 100°F (39°C), pleasant enough on a beach but unbearable when you're trudging round the sights. New York heat is especially tiring because of the high humidity. Wake up, shower, step out on to the street and you will be needing a second shower within the hour. The only reprieve is to keep slipping into air-conditioned stores or even a bookshop, just to flick the pages to fan your face. Unfortunately, the summer nights are rarely cool, so even a sheet feels too heavy at night. At weekends sensible New Yorkers tend to get out, the beaches on Long Island being especially popular. In winter the weather does an about turn. By December, January and February temperatures are down to the 30s°F and 40s°F (0 to 10°C), sometimes dropping to freezing, and icy winds whistle around the blocks, sometimes accompanied by snow. But even though the mercury is barely climbing out of the bulb, New York's winter days often mean blue skies and sunshine, perfect for sightseeing as long as you wrap up.

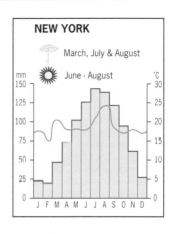

NEW YORK

March, July & August

June - August

What to Wear

To combat the heat of summer, New Yorkers tend to overdo the air-conditioning in hotels, restaurants and taxis, so between June and September it is always wise to carry a light sweater for use indoors! In winter, dress in plenty of layers on top of your thermals – you will find radiators turned up to unhealthy proportions. At any time a raincoat is a wise item to pack, or at least an umbrella. Since New York weather forecasts are pretty accurate you can plan your day's wear accordingly without over- or under-doing it. Many restaurants in the US go in for 'dress codes', but New York is a lot less formal in this respect than say, the mid-West. Only the more chic restaurants require a jacket and tie. At the pricey end of the scale denim, T-shirts and other casual clothes may be frowned upon at some of the smarter restaurants, discos and nightclubs.

HOW TO BE A LOCAL

There are New Yorkers and
New Yorkers. The style of
speech is often to the point,
rationally expressed, and
without polite embellishments,
especially between strangers.
Visitors who are used to effusive
apologies and courtesies often
misconstrue this as rudeness.
As often as not it is just people
being very articulate, quick of
tongue and to the point. In fact,
in some ways they are *more*
polite than Europeans. If they
accidentally bump into you on
the street they will always offer
an 'excuse me' – even if you did
the bumping. There are
exceptions. Once roused, a New
York tongue is liable to let fly
with the most original and quick-
witted insults you will ever hear
in your life. Taxi drivers either

*The key to being a local is, as
always, to play it by ear!*

can't stop the flow of words
(loquacious turbo models) or sit
like morose hulks who will not
even grunt to your 'Good
morning'. The chances are that
they are newly immigrated and
don't speak English. In such
instances, be ready to offer at
least rudimentary directions to
your destination.
However well they may speak
English, typical New Yorkers
never talk in whispers or with
pauses and see no reason to
deviate from this norm even
when they are eating. To gain
strength for the day, New Yorkers
(assuming they are not on a
health kick) breakfast early at
their local diner on calories and
caffeine. This gives them strength
to face the ups and downs of the
New York day and, fortified by a
noisy lunch, for standing in line
for hours outside a dinner
restaurant deemed fashionable
– or just better than average – in
the latest press reviews.
Local tips:
● Tip generously.
● Use the subway (but avoid
rush hours) or walk.
● Houston Street is pronounced
Howston: you are not in Texas.
● Ask for directions and expect
to receive them in terms of
'blocks' – plots of land defined
by the intersections of streets
and avenues.
● Americans don't use the terms
'loo' or 'toilet'. Ask for the
washroom, bathroom or
restroom'.
● Don't react violently to a
soapy chamois leather suddenly
appearing on your windscreen
in a traffic jam: it's common
entrepreneurial practice by
unemployed youths to 'offer'

their windscreen cleaning services, though if you prefer to screech off in a cloud of Windolene that's up to you.

PERSONAL PRIORITIES

New York, with exceptions, is a very openly heterosexual city. Since there is a high ratio of single people, there is more *frisson* in the air than in many other cities. And it is not only the men who do the chasing. But women will still find workers on building sites giving wolf-whistles in between bits of the lunchtime sandwiches. And there are a lot of crazy people in the city, so precautions about avoiding dark alleys, locking hotel/apartment doors and not opening them until you are sure of the identity of the caller, really are vitally important.

The gay scene is quite open here. Christopher Street is still the focal point, both for residents living in the West Village and for weekend out-of-towners, but the atmosphere is far less hedonistic than in pre-Aids days. Nonetheless, specifically gay-and lesbian-aimed magazines, and more mainstream ones such as the *Village Voice*, carry extensive listings for gay and lesbian clubs (often an otherwise straight club which is gay or lesbian on certain nights of the week). Some clubs are exclusively male or female although most welcome straight friends of gays or lesbians. The few surviving hardcore leather and S&M bars and clubs, welcome participants but not voyeurs. The no-go areas of New York are not to do with sexual

inclinations but financial deprivations. Spanish Harlem, South Bronx and the Bedford Stuyvesant area of Brooklyn are to be treated with extreme caution by day and avoided at night. Some people avoid the subway at night but others would say that this is unnecessary provided you board at busy stations (using the supervised 'off-hours' waiting area) and sit in an occupied carriage of the train.

CHILDREN

New York's reputation as a haven of crime, drugs and commerce does nothing to encourage families to pay a visit. Yet, contrary to popular belief, New York is an ideal city for kids. Not only do many of its attractions welcome children and provide facilities especially for them, but the shop windows also overflow with clothes, with brand name items such as Osh Kosh and Heath-Tex often at very reasonable prices. Neon-lit fast food joints have menus beyond the coke, hamburger and milkshake repertoire and there's the whole of Central Park for letting off steam. On wet days there is always the TV, with cartoons on every other channel (so it will seem to grown-ups), plus a huge zoo in the Bronx (a smaller one in Central Park), baseball games in Shea Stadium, the toys in FAO Schwarz, and so on. It would be hard for any child not to feel he has landed in paradise.
For full listings details of the entertainments on hand, refer to the *New York Times*.

CHILDREN

Babysitting

The Babysitters Guild, 60 East 42nd Street (tel: 682 0227), is one of the best agencies, with an unbeatable reputation. All the staff work for a minimum of four hours. Babies up to six months cost more because your babysitter will be a trained nurse.

Other good babysitting agencies include:
Stern College for Women, 245 Lexington Avenue (tel: 340 7715) and **Barnard College Babysitting Service**, 606 West 120th Street (tel: 280 2035).

Museums

Aunt Len's Doll and Toy Museum, 6 Hamilton Terrace (tel: 926 4172). A delightful collection of 3,000 or so dolls and teddy bears collected by schoolteacher 'Aunt Len'. Visitors should phone for an appointment.

Brooklyn Children's Museum, 145 Brooklyn Avenue (tel: 718 735 4400). Claims to be the world's first children's museum (founded 1899), with lots of hands-on exhibits. Parents can enjoy it too.

Open: Monday to Friday 14.00-17.00hrs; weekends and holidays 10.00-17.00hrs.

Children's Museum of Manhattan, 212 West 83rd Street (tel: 721 1223). Art, culture, science and nature exhibits, for ages two to 12.

Open: Tuesday to Sunday 10.00-17.00hrs (June-August); Monday, Wednesday-Friday 13.00-17.00 and weekends 10.00-17.00hrs (rest of year).

Museum of Television and Radio 25 West 52nd Street (tel: 621 6800). Choose from 20,000 TV and radio programmes (new and old) and sit and watch them for up to an hour. Includes *Rin Tin Tin* and *The Lone Ranger*.

Open: Tuesday to Sunday noon-18.00hrs (Thursday until 20.00hrs; Friday until 21.00hrs).

South Street Seaport, on the East River, at the foot of Fulton Street. Daily street entertainment throughout the summer, featuring musicians, puppeteers, jugglers and mimes. Inside the **South Street Seaport Museum**, 207 Front Street (tel: 669 9400/9424), is a children's centre with lots of activities. Under-4's get in free (open daily 10.00-17.00hrs).

Staten Island Children's Museum, 1000 Richmond Terrace, Snug Harbor (tel: 718 273 2060). Pride of place among imaginative exhibits is the Clockworks Sound Arcade. Concerts are held in the building on weekends and school holidays.

Open: Tuesday to Sunday noon–17.00hrs.

Other adult museums which have special children's programmes include the **American Museum of Natural History**, Central Park West at 79th Street (tel: 769 5800), whose lifesize dinosaurs are particularly popular, along with the laser rock shows at the Hayden Planetarium next door; the **Museum of Holography**, 11 Mercer Street (tel: 925 0526); and the **Metropolitan Museum of Art**, 1000 Fifth

Looking out for children's needs: the Museum of Natural History

Avenue at 82nd Street (tel: 535 7710), which has a Junior Museum with challenging but comprehensible exhibitions mainly aimed at five to 12 year olds.

Out and About
Astroland (Coney Island). West 10th Street between Surf Avenue and Coney Island Boardwalk, Coney Island, Brooklyn (tel: 718 372 0275). Thirty years ago this was considered *the* amusement park in America for the working classes. It's now a shadow of its former self, fraying at the edges and more than a little rough at the seams, though you can still catch the Cyclone, the legendary roller coaster, pitch softballs, drive bumper cars, have your picture stamped on a T-shirt, spin in Hell Hole, walk on the boardwalk and wash down a

hot dog from the original Nathan's stand with a beer; and the beach still has fine yellow sand (open daily, noon to midnight, mid-June to mid-September). Follow a visit with a meal at one of many seafood waterfront restaurants on Emmons Avenue, opposite the fishing boats in the docks. To get to Coney Island take the B, D, F or N trains to the end of the line from Manhattan (an hour's ride).
Big Apple Circus. There's no set date for this tented extravaganza – you have to check listings for advance warning (or call 268 0055). It usually appears in summer and over Christmas at, for example, Damrosch Park in the Lincoln Center, and costs very little as a non-profit making enterprise. All the traditional cavorters are represented, including clowns, aerialists, trapeze artists, acrobats and musicians.
Central Park. On the back of

the map at the entrances is a calendar which lists events, several of them for children, including nature walks by Urban Park Rangers, exhibits at the Dairy, storytelling at the Hans Christian Andersen statue and boating on the lake.

Putter's Paradise. 48 West 21st Street (tel: 727-PUTT). An 18-hole miniature golf course set in a gargantuan tropical setting with bubble-gum pink walls, flamingoes, trees, and a bunch of rotating bananas.
Open: Wednesday and Thursday 18.00hrs-midnight, Friday and Saturday 17.30-01.00hrs; Sunday 17.30-20.00hrs.

A **Circle Line Boat Tour**, Pier 83, West 42nd Street (tel: 563 3200), takes three hours around Manhattan Island, a little long for under fives, but otherwise one big thrill. Children under 12 pay half price. Boats leave regularly throughout the day from March to December. The

Spot the ball...the Yankee Stadium in the Bronx

Staten Island ferry from Battery Park is equally exciting, with lots of room for children to run around on deck.

Sports
Most teenage children will find being a spectator at a baseball game by the Yankees or the Mets wildly exciting. The Mets play at Shea Stadium in Flushing, Queens (tel: 718 507 8499), the Yankees at their stadium in the Bronx (tel: 293 6000).

Theatres
Phone for details of plays, fairy tale telling and musicals at the following theatres:
Courtyard Playhouse, 39 Grove Street (tel: 765 9540).
First All Children's Theater, 37 West 65th Street, near Central Park West (tel: 873 6400).
Magic Towne House, 1026

Third Avenue, near 60th Street (tel: 752 1165).

Thirteenth Street Theater, 50 West 13th Street (tel: 675 6677).

Truck and Warehouse Theater, 79 East Fourth Street, near Second Avenue (tel: 254 5060), which features a long-running musical, *Captain Boogie and the Kids from Mars*, performed weekends only between October and June.

The **American Symphony Orchestra** and the **New York Philharmonic** sometimes perform concerts of classical music for children aged between six and 16. Most are scheduled over the autumn/winter period at Carnegie Hall (tel: 247 7800) or Avery Fisher Hall in the Lincoln Center (tel: 874 2424).

Traditional Sights

The sights most suited to parents with children in tow include the **Statue of Liberty**, the **Empire State Building, World Trade Center** and Rockefeller Center's **GE Building**. Their Observation Decks always instill a feeling of awe. The pedestrian walkway along the **Brooklyn Bridge** is another children's favourite. **Radio City Music Hall** is designed for family entertainment: the backstage tours offer an insight into an exciting world for youngsters. If you happen to be in the Big Apple over Christmas the most dazzling light displays are on the 70-foot (21m) tree at the base of the GE Building, midtown Fifth Avenue, and the windows of shops like Saks Fifth Avenue, FAO Schwarz (the best

toy shop in town, which holds free puppet shows from Monday to Friday at 14.30hrs) and Lord & Taylor. Most exciting of the city's annual parades for children are St Patrick's Day Parade on 17 March and Macy's Thanksgiving Day Parade on the last Thursday in November: the Disney-style balloons are absolutely gigantic.

Zoos

Bronx Zoo, Fordham Road at Bronx River Parkway, the Bronx (tel: 367 1010 for information and directions). The US's largest urban zoo is set in 265 acres (107 hectares) of woods, ponds, streams and parkland. Thousands of creatures include bullfrogs and bison, cheetahs and cranes, egrets and elephants, panthers and peafowl. Specialised exhibitions include the World of Darkness (nocturnal animals), Jungle World (indoor tropical house), World of Birds, Wild Asia and the newly opened Children's Zoo opposite the elephant house. When your shoes and energy start to wear out, hop on the Safari Train, the Skyfari aerial tramway or the Bengall Express, a narrated monorail which takes you through the open meadows and dark forests of Wild Asia. Camel rides are also available. *Open:* daily, 10.00-17.00hrs (weekends until 17.30hrs) closing at 16.30hrs daily November to March. Admission by donation (except Wednesday).

Central Park Zoo, Central Park, 64th Street and Fifth Avenue (tel: 861 6030). The Children's Zoo is open from 10.00 to 17.00hrs daily.

New York Aquarium, Surf Avenue and West Eighth Street, Coney Island, Brooklyn (tel: 718 265 FISH). Twelve thousand gallon tanks are filled with coral and fish. Children can discover how animals hear under water, and stand beneath a 400-gallon wave. Frequent shows performed by the belugas (white whales). Also dolphins, seals, penguins, sealions. Down the boardwalk is Coney Island's amusement park (Astroland) with Cyclone roller coaster.

Open: daily 10.00-16.45hrs (17.00hrs weekends and summer holidays).

Washington Square, in the heart of Greenwich Village, hosts an open-air art exhibition in late spring and early autumn

TIGHT BUDGET

It's not unheard of to be stopped by a tramp in New York and asked if you can spare $100. But despite the fact that New York ranks amongst the world's most exorbitant cities, it is still possible to do the sights, enjoy the shops, see the shows and rub shoulders with the rich and famous without breaking the bank, as long as you know where to look for the bargains.

The New York Convention and Visitors Bureau publishes a *20 Free Things to Do in New York City* fact sheet.

Accommodation

A cheap place to stay is hard to find in New York. There are a few, however, listed in the budget section of **Accommodation**, page 85.

Atriums

The atriums of many of the city's skyscrapers are landscaped sights in themselves, with plunging waterfalls, lush foliage and spectacular architecture. They serve as art galleries-cum-restaurants-cum-shops-cum-resting-between-sights spots. The world's largest indoor atrium is in the Marriott Marquis hotel on Times Square; Trump Tower's indoor street is paved and walled with rose-pink marble and bronze, five storeys of boutiques, restaurants and cafés and an 80-foot (24m) waterfall under a glass and brass skylight. The Equitable Center's atrium is a recent addition to the city's art scene with Roy Lichtenstein's huge *Mural with Blue Brushstroke* dominating the arched entrance, and changing exhibits from the Whitney's collection of 20th-century art. Other impressive atriums include the Citicorp Center (53rd Street, between Third and Lexington Avenues), IBM Garden Plaza (56th Street at Madison Avenue), Rockefeller Center (49th to 50th Streets at Fifth Avenue), Park Avenue Atrium (45th to 46th Streets, between Park and Lexington) and the Winter Garden in the World Financial Center.

Culture

'Pay anything as long as it's something' are the instructions in many of New York's museums and galleries. The American Craft Museum, Cooper-Hewitt and the International Center of Photography offer completely free entry on Tuesday evenings. The Whitney Museum of American Art is free on Thursday evenings. The American Museum of Natural History is free Friday and Saturday nights, while the Guggenheim offers cheaper entry on Tuesday evenings. City Gallery (closed July and August), Forbes Magazine Galleries, IBM Gallery of Science and Art, Lever House and the Whitney Museum at Philip Morris, Equitable Center is always free. For browsing there is the Place des Antiquaires on East 57th Street, an international art and antiques centre, luxuriously hollowed out with marble walls and pillars. For animal lovers the Bronx Zoo is free on Wednesdays and by donation at other times.

For New York's trendiest art galleries, head for SoHo, where the renovated lofts and gargantuan warehouses open their doors for free.

Outdoor art includes *Sylvette*, Picasso's colossal sculpture in Greenwich Village on Bleecker Street; the Vietnam Veterans Memorial at 55 Water Street; and Bernard Rosenthal's giant black cube in Astor Place. The Washington Square-Greenwich Village outdoor art exhibition takes place during a weekend early in June. Besides the various summer festivals, free open air music in parks, subways, building lobbies and street corners is an essential ingredient of the New York summer. Places include Cooper-Hewitt Museum, the Museum of Modern Art's

Summer Garden, St Paul's Chapel, World Trade Center Plaza, Trinity Church and Washington Square Park. You can also catch the Metropolitan Opera in Central Park and in the New York Botanical Garden, and the New York Grand Opera in Central Park's 72nd Street Bandshell. The New York Philharmonic holds free performances in Central Park, plus parks in Brooklyn, Queens, Staten Island and the Bronx with fireworks (tel: 580 8700). For raunchier rhythms, Brooklyn's parks are a continual Notting Hill Carnival of jazz, classical, Latin, Afro-Caribbean and steel bands throughout July and August.

Free music, dance and theatre events are also staged in the parks and plazas of the Lincoln Center throughout August (for details of the daily schedule of events tel: 877 2011).

Summerpier concerts at South Street Seaport, again free of charge, are held on Fridays and Saturdays at 19.30hrs in July and August (tel: 669 9424). Churches and cathedrals contain some impressive works of art and architecture. Try the Cathedral of St John the Divine, St Patrick's Cathedral, Riverside Church, St Bartholomew's Church, Temple Emanu-El, Trinity Church and St Paul's Chapel.

Discount Cards

An International Student ID card can often guarantee a discount, and the noticeboards of the city's colleges and universities are a mine of information on free or budget activities. Senior citizens, juniors, honeymooners, journalists, government employees, teachers and groups are often entitled to special rates in hotels, museums, sightseeing attractions, restaurants and clubs.

Getting Around

For a relatively short journey, New York's yellow cabs are cheaper for several people sharing than taking the subway. Free bus and subway maps are available from all stations. But the cheapest way of all is to walk.

Nightlife

Many nightclubs can be entered free of charge. The Limelight, Tunnel and 10.18, for example, give out free passes to shops in Greenwich Village and SoHo (especially those situated on Lower Broadway and Seventh Avenue). Alternatively, ask any New Yorkers you know (or have met) if you could have their passes; most are on mailing lists for various clubs and often receive tickets with an open bar facility for various 'theme' nights.

Details of clubs and venues can be found in the *Village Voice* which comes out every Wednesday.

Shopping

The best shopping bargains are Levis and T-shirts, and sports and outdoor gear like backpacks, trainers and track suits. Bargain-hunters should try the Lower East Side Orchard Street market on Sundays, West 14th Street (between Fifth and Seventh), Unique Clothing Warehouse at 718 Broadway and Alice Underground, a second-hand clothing emporium on Columbus Avenue at 78th.

Sightseeing

The 40-minute round trip on the Staten Island ferry is a bargain. It lets you set foot in another borough and offers a spectacular view of the Statue of Liberty and the Lower Manhattan skyline, for 50 cents. Sights to spot *en route* besides an impressive view of Downtown Manhattan's architecture, are the gargantuan Colgate clock in Jersey City, New Jersey, the Verrazano Narrows Bridge, and the *QEII* cruise liner. There are free landmark tours of Grand Central Terminal on Wednesdays at 12.30hrs (meet under the Kodak sign) and of New York Public Library (5th Avenue and 42nd Street) Monday to Saturday at 11.00 and 14.00hrs.

But the cheapest way to sightsee is to cruise the streets on foot. Go up Columbus Avenue and down Amsterdam Avenue on the Upper West Side of town, for example, and you will have covered the majority of the city's newest yuppie stores and restaurants. Cross Brooklyn Bridge at dusk and turn back for a stunning view of Manhattan. Combine Greenwich Village with the less touristy West and East Villages, then continue down to SoHo.

Other sights best seen from the street include South Street Seaport (the restored historic maritime core of New York). From here it's only a minute's walk to Wall Street and the window ledges where high financiers jumped to their deaths after the 1929 crash. See the Stock Exchange floor for free from the public gallery. Other free sights include Times Square, the art deco Chrysler Building and the Dakota building on Central Park West, site of John Lennon's assasination. Pick up a free self-guided Rockefeller Center walking tour brochure from the Visitors Bureau and discover the Center's art deco bas reliefs and outdoor sculpture, as well as the Channel Gardens, which separate the British and French Buildings on Fifth Avenue between 49th and 50th Streets.

Parks and gardens such as Brooklyn Botanic Gardens and New York Botanical Garden in the Bronx are open free daily. On Saturdays the Crystal Palace Haupt Conservatory (New York Botanical Garden) is free between 10.00hrs and midday.

Theatre

Even a night at the theatre is within reach of the impoverished. Half-price tickets are sold (on the day of performance) for Broadway and Off Broadway shows at the TKTS booth in Times Square. Matinée seats go on sale at

10.00hrs, evening seats at 15.00hrs. There is another booth in the lobby of 2 World Trade Center, open Monday to Friday 11.00-17.30hrs; Saturday until 15.30hrs and at Court and Montague Streets, Brooklyn (same hours as the World Travel Trade Center, but closed Mondays). (Off Broadway 11.00-13.00hrs only). Matinée and Sunday tickets are sold one day prior to performance date. The Visitors Bureau Information Centers also distribute 'twofers', discount theatre coupons, plus free tickets to TV shows on a daily basis. The Music and Dance Booth in Bryant Park at 42nd Street offers half-price day-of-performance tickets for music and dance events (closed Monday, tickets for this day are sold on Sunday). Visit the neighbourhood street

Street festivals highlight the city's rich cultural mix

festivals, which are free, easy and highly entertaining. The best include Chinese New Year (January/February), Ninth Avenue Festival (May), Queens Festival (June), Harlem Day (August), West Indian Day (Labor Day, September), La Festa di San Gennaro (September) and Greenwich Village Hallowe'en Parade (31 October).

Where to Eat
Hamburgers and hot dogs aside, the only way to eat cheaply in New York is to eat ethnic. Start off with a breakfast in one of the many Greek-run coffee shops, a mid-morning mega-sized pastrami sandwich lunch at Katz's Deli (East Houston Street) or a *Dim Sum* in Chinatown, follow it up with a Creole dinner at Miss Ruby's Café (135 Eighth Avenue) and round the evening off with a *sambucca* in Little Italy, to give you a taste of the huge range on offer at low prices.

SPECIAL EVENTS
January/February
Chinese New Year: the new 12 moons of the Chinese calendar begin in late January or early February, with festivals and festivities in Chinatown.

March
St Patrick's Day Parade: along Fifth Avenue, over the weekend nearest 17 March. Best, though crowded, place for viewing is St Patrick's Cathedral.
Greek Independence Day Parade: 25 March, unless it falls in the Orthodox Lent, in which case the date is moved on to April or May. The parade

moves down Fifth Avenue and ends up in 49th Street.

March/April
Easter Parade: one of the city's biggest carnivals is on Fifth Avenue on Easter Friday. A colourful spectacle of floats, balloons and flowers. During the week preceding Easter the floors of Macy's are strewn with spectacular flower arrangements.

May
Ninth Avenue International Food Festival: held in May, an infamous diet-buster, as delis and restaurants display their wares from 37th to 57th Streets. Take an enormous appetite to sample the cuisines of at least 20 nationalities.

June
Feast of St Anthony: an Italian extravaganza held in early June in Sullivan Street, Greenwich Village over ten days. Its climax is a band procession, with locals carrying a huge lookalike of a saint.

Puerto Rican Day Parade: a patriotic musical bash on the second Sunday in June along Fifth Avenue.

Bronx Week: the Bronx district melts into parades, dancing, theatre events and concerts for a week in early June.

Lower East Side Jewish Spring Festival: the second Sunday in June on East Broadway between Rutgers and Montgomery Streets. Lots of kosher foods to try, plus Yiddish and Hebrew entertainment.

Gay Pride March: on 24 June the city's gay community remembers the Stonewall riots

of 1969 and subsequent achievements.

Harbor Festival: maritime and sporting events at the end of June until early August, including the Stars and Stripes Regatta in New York Harbor. Liberty Cup yacht races held off South Street Seaport.

July
American Independence Day: 4 July means festivities all over America. In New York, join the festivities along Water Street from Battery Park to John Street. Macy's climatic fireworks along the East River are best enjoyed from Riverside Park from around 21.00hrs.

NY Summer Festival of Theater and Music: hundreds of events throughout July. Details from the New York Convention and Visitors Bureau.

September
Labor Day Parade: down Fifth Avenue early September.
Festa di San Gennaro: a predominantly Little Italy celebration held for 10 days from the week of 9 September. A model of the saint is paraded through the streets festooned in dollar bills.

October
Hallowe'en: 31 October. Always taken seriously by American children, who hollow out pumpkins and roam the streets asking 'trick or treats'. Best place to celebrate is Greenwich Village, where there is a Hallowe'en Parade.

November
Macy's Thanksgiving Day

SPECIAL EVENTS/SPORT

Parade: Central Park West from 77th to 59th Street, down Broadway to 34th Street. As big an event as Christmas; the entire city takes a holiday and sits down to a turkey dinner on the last Thursday in November.

December/January
New Year's Eve: celebrations are focused on Times Square.

SPORT

New Yorkers adore watching sports, even more than taking part in them. Top of the popularity league is baseball, though American football and basketball come close seconds. You will find sports coverage in the *Times* on Tuesdays, the *News* and the *Post* daily.

American Football
For most of the year (high summer being the only exception) there is a good chance of finding the faces in a neighbourhood bar tuned into one corner, avidly watching the latest football game. New York's teams are the Jets, who play at **Shea Stadium**, 126th Street at Roosevelt Avenue, Queens (tel: 507 8499), and the NY Giants, based at **Meadowland Sports Complex**, East Rutherford, New Jersey (tel: 201 935 8111). Regular buses from Port Authority Bus Terminal on 42nd Street and Eighth Avenue.

Baseball
If the legendary names of baseball (Babe Ruth, Lou Gehrig, Joe Di Maggio, Mickey Mantle, Roger Maris, etc), mean

anything to you, visit **Yankee Stadium**, East 161st Street and River Avenue, the Bronx (tel: 293 6000), where their ghosts live on. The Yankee pinstripes play ball, often floodlit, in 'the house that Ruth built' from April to October (subway: CC, D or 4 to 161st Station).
The NY Mets play at Shea Stadium, and it would be a philistine indeed who wasn't caught up in the infectious enthusiasm of 55,000 people watching the 'Orange and Blues' screaming 'Let's Go Mets!' (*subway*: 7 to Willets Point/Shea Stadium Station).

Basketball
The NY Knickerbockers (Knicks) play regularly from October to June at **Madison Square Garden**, West 33rd Street and Seventh Avenue (tel: 465 6741). Variously billed as New York's Roman Colisseum, the Central Palace of Pleasure or even the Center of the Universe, MSG is also the home ground for the Rangers ice hockey team. Bjorn Borg has played here, Mohammed Ali's been stung, Billy Graham evangelised and Marilyn Monroe once rode a pink elephant here (*subway*: 1, 2 and 3 to 34th Street Penn Stadium).

Horseracing
Followers of the turf can try the off-track betting for harness and thoroughbred horseracing at the **Aqueduct Raceway**, Ozone Park, Rockaway, Queens, and **Belmont Park** on Long Island (information: 718 704 5148). Races take place between January and May, and during June and July. For details of

Around-the-clock jogging is a top pastime – along with eating

tickets that include transport to the tracks, call 718 330 1234 or ask at Grand Central Terminal for Aqueduct, Penn Station for Belmont Park.

Ice Skating
Though skimming along the frozen wastes is associated with rural rivers and lakes, New Yorkers make excellent use of sub-zero winter temperatures. The rink in the **Rockefeller Center** (tel: 757 5730) is the most popular, followed by the rink in Central Park. Otherwise try **Kate Wollman Rink** in Prospect Park, Brooklyn (tel: 718 965 6561).

Jogging
Arguably the second favourite pastime, after eating. The most popular place is Central Park, particularly anti-clockwise around Receiving Reservoir. Also Riverside Park or along the banks of the East River. The jogging event of the year is the New York Marathon in October. The 26-mile (41km) course starts in Staten Island, crosses the Verrazano-Narrows Bridge and winds through all the outer boroughs, puffing to an exhausted close at the Tavern on the Green in Central Park. Entry forms from **Road Runners Club**, PO Box 881, FDR Station, New York, NY 10150 (tel: 860 4455).

Swimming
There are several city-owned gymnasium and pool complexes. Addresses include 59th Street and West End Avenue (tel: 397 3170); 35 West 134th Street (tel: 397 3193); Clarkson Street and Seventh Avenue (tel: 397 3147); and 342 East 54th Street (tel: 397 3148).

Tennis
The main event is the US Open Championships, held in Queens during the last two weeks of August at the **USTA National Tennis Center**, Flushing Meadow (tel: 718 592 8000). Beware exorbitant ticket prices.

DIRECTORY

Arriving

Visas are not required by British citizens with full right of abode in the UK, or nationals of Canada, France, Germany, Italy, the Netherlands, Sweden and Switzerland visiting for business or tourist purposes for a stay of up to 90 days. provided they hold an unexpired passport and a non-refundable, non-transferrable return ticket issued by a participating carrier.

You will be asked to complete a visa waiver form on the airline/ship. Visitors from Australia and New Zealand require a visa. Should you need a visa, send the application form (available from travel agents and the American Embassy) to the American Embassy visa department of your country (see **Embassies and Consulates**, page 118, for addresses). Allow at least two weeks, more if possible. All babies and children should be included on their parents' passport, but young visitors from the UK do not require a visa as long as the parents complete a visa waiver form for them.

There are three airports in New York: JF Kennedy International and La Guardia (mainly domestic flights), both in Queens, and Newark International in New Jersey. The Port Authority of New York and New Jersey has a free information service for transportation to and from all three airports (tel: 800 247 7433).

Fly into New York City and become one of the jet setters!

115

DIRECTORY

Airport Transfers

JFK: 16 miles (26km) from mid-Manhattan. An Express Bus runs to the Carey Bus ticket office, 125 Park Avenue (near Grand Central Terminal) every 20 minutes between 06.00 and midnight from Grand Central and between 05.00hrs and 00.30hrs from JFK. Journey time: 60-75 minutes (additional information: 718 632 0500).

An Express Bus also runs every hour (07.00-19.00hrs) from Williamsburgh Bank, 1 Hanson Place, Williamsburg, Brooklyn and every 30 minutes (06.00-23.00hrs) from Long Island Rail Road Station in Jamaica, Sutphin Boulevard and Archer Avenue in Queens.

The JFK Express 'train to plane' service runs every 20 minutes between 05.00hrs and midnight (tel: 718 858 7272), and takes 70 minutes. Arriving passengers take the free shuttle bus to the Howard Beach Station, where they catch the subway to Brooklyn and Manhattan.

Public buses (marked Q-10 and operated by Green Bus Lines, tel: 718 995 4700) run from JFK terminals to subway stations at Lefferts Boulevard (for trains to Brooklyn, Lower and West Side Manhattan) and Kew Gardens-Union Turnpike (for trains to Queens and mid-Manhattan). Buses run about every 10 minutes between 06.30 and 19.00hrs and every 20-30 minutes from 19.00 to 06.30hrs. Buses marked Q-3 (operated by the New York Transit Authority tel: 718 330 1234) run from JFK terminals to 179th Street for connections to

Manhattan and Brooklyn. Every 12-15 minutes, between 05.25 and 21.25 hrs and every 30 minutes from 21.45 to 01.45 hrs; weekends every 20-30 minutes.

A taxi to midtown Manhattan takes around an hour.

A helicopter service (10-minute flight) operates every 30 minutes between JFK and the heliport at 34th Street at the East River or the World Trade Center heliport, 14.30 to 19.30hrs (tel: 800 645 3494).

Newark: 15 miles (24km) from Manhattan. Transfer time to Manhattan also tends to be quicker than from JFK: around 40 minutes.

A round-the-clock Express Bus (New Jersey Transit) runs between Newark and Manhattan every 15 or 20 minutes (tel: 201 762 5100) from New York; free phone 800 772 2222 from New Jersey. A similar airlink express bus, Olympia Trails, costs the same and runs from Newark Airport to Penn Station or Grand Central Terminal every 20 minutes between 06.15hrs and midnight or to the World Trade Center every 20/30 minutes between 06.00 and 22.00hrs (information tel: 964 6233).

Taxis are hard to get for the trip into town, and also charge more than for JFK because they are New Jersey licensed. A cheaper alternative is a shared minibus: **Abbey's Transportation** (tel: 718 361 9092) provide a service to major Manhattan hotels.

La Guardia: Express Bus departs from Carey Bus ticket office

DIRECTORY

(near Grand Central Terminal) every 20 minutes between 06.45hrs and midnight. Journey time: 30-45 minutes. A shuttle bus picks up at the AirTrans Center in Port Authority Bus Terminal every 30 minutes from 07.15 to 21.45hrs (additional information: 718 632 0500/9). Connections from Brooklyn and Queens are the same as for JFK, except every 30 minutes from Brooklyn. Public buses (marked Q-33 and operated Triboro) operate between La Guardia's main terminal and the 74th Street subway station in Queens, with connections to Manhattan. Buses run around the clock, every 12 minutes, or about every 40 minutes after midnight. (Additional information: 718 335 1000.) The Water Shuttle departs every 40 minutes from Pier II, South and Wall Streets, every 25 minutes from 34th and East River, to La Guardia Marine Air Terminal (details of weekday schedule: 800 543 3779). Taxis take around 30 minutes to midtown Manhattan.

Chemist see Pharmacist

Crime

New York has a reputation for being hard, fast and dangerous. But, as in any large city, your chances of becoming one of the victim statistics has a good deal to do with acting sensibly. Don't take the subway after midnight on your own; don't walk on quiet streets alone at night (it's illegal to enter Central Park on foot after dark); and only visit deprived areas like Harlem on a guided tour. Carry only the cash you need on any one sortie from your hotel, leaving the rest with the desk for safe keeping, and don't display unnecessary jewellery and other valuables. In the event of a crime such as theft or mugging, hail a cab and ask to be taken to the nearest police station. They will probably be able to do little more than sympathise, but at least you will receive a reference to hand to your insurance company.

Customs Regulations

For non-US residents over 21 the duty free allowance is 200 cigarettes, or 50 cigars or 2kg tobacco or any proportionate combination, one US quart of spirits or wine and up to $100 duty free gifts (including up to 100 cigars), providing the stay in the US is at least 72 hours and that the gift exemption has not been claimed in the previous six months. Prohibited goods include meat and meat products, dairy products, plants, fruits, seeds, drugs, lottery tickets and obscene publications.

Driving

Nobody drives in Manhattan unless it is absolutely essential. Parking is a major problem: either very expensive in public car parks or almost impossible on the streets of Manhattan. Local residents cruising round and round their home blocks in search of a slot is one of the city's more idiosyncratic sights.

If you must drive a car into New York City (which is often congested) it is vital that you

Consider joining a guided tour to visit deprived areas of New York such as Harlem

read the parking restriction signs very carefully or be prepared to pay for a meter or parking lot; which are costly and difficult to find. Fees and penalties are fierce, and the privately operated tow-away services are faster than anywhere, because they work on a commission basis. The city enforces an alternate-side-of-the-street parking law: you cannot leave your car in a space for more than one night. It is illegal to park within 10 feet (3.3m) either side of fire hydrants, even if there is no warning sign. Your car will be towed away, and you will receive a hefty fine. It goes without saying that you should not leave *anything* in your vehicle unguarded.

Breakdowns: members of motoring organisations affiliated to the AAA (American Automobile Association) can get its services free of charge. Help is readily available from the efficient Highway Patrols. Just wait by the car, perhaps attaching a white handkerchief to the radio aerial. If it is a hired car, call the rental company and tell them about the breakdown.

Car rental: there are hundreds of car rental companies ranging from the multinational giants to the small back street operators, and even those who specialise in renting old wrecks at highly competitive rates. Prices are generally extremely competitive and it pays to shop around, since different ones offer special discounts for, say, weekend travel, when their main business customers have gone home. Expect to pay for unlimited mileage but not Collision Damage Waiver or Personal Accident insurance. Special weekend deals are widely available. Many

DIRECTORY

companies will not rent to under 25s. A full valid national EC driving licence is acceptable, or an International driving permit.

The main car hire companies are:

Avis (tel: 331 1212)
Budget (tel: 527 0700)
Dollar (tel: 399 3590)
Greyhound (tel: 327 2501)
Hertz (tel: 654 3131)
Interrent (tel: 227 7368)
National (tel: 227 7368)
Thrifty (tel: 367 2277)

All the above numbers are toll free and should be prefaced by dialling 800.

Two things to note when driving in New York are that traffic lights turn from red to green with no amber; you may also find your windscreen being washed whether you like it or not at a traffic junction. New Yorkers are brazen to this behaviour by unemployed youths and either let them get on with it and pay a dollar or so accordingly, or say no and drive off as soon as the lights change.

Fuel: five American gallons equal approximately four Imperial gallons or 18 litres. Most late-night and 24-hour gas (petrol) stations require you to pay the cashier before filling commences.

Laws: drive on the right, but use miles rather than kilometres. Driving while intoxicated (DWI) is a very serious offence. Alcohol must be kept in the boot. The speed limit all over the US is 55mph (88kph), although a few states (including New York) have upped the level to 65mph

(104kph) on highways. Radar is used extensively out of town and you will not get away with exceeding the limit. In New York the limit is 20-25mph (32-40kph) depending on the area, though few motorists take heed of this, especially cab and truck drivers. Always stop behind a stationary school bus (usually yellow) with flashing indicators.

Tolls: turnpikes, the freeway toll booths, give you a distance card when you enter. You pay the charge when you reach the exit. There is also a charge on some expressways, bridges and tunnels (around $2.50), so keep some change handy.

Upstate: outside New York the Interstate Highways are thousands of miles long. They bear the letter 'I' (for Interstate) plus a number. They are marked on maps and signs with a red, white and blue shield. If you miss your exit, never turn round, no matter how far the next exit.

Electricity

110/120 volts AC (60 cycles). Sockets take two/flat-pin plugs.

Embassies and Consulates

American Embassies abroad:
Australia: Moonhah Place, Canberra (tel: 062 733 711).
New Zealand: 29 Fitzherbert Terrace, Thorndon, Wellington (tel: 04 722 068).
UK: 24 Grosvenor Square, London. W1A 1AE (tel: 071 499 9000).
Visa Unit: 5 Upper Grosvenor Street, London W1A 2JB (tel: 071 499 7010/3443).

Emergency Telephone Numbers

Police, fire brigade or ambulance: 911 (for immediate medical care dial 496 9620). Emergency dentist: 679 3966. Local police: check in the phone book for local precinct or contact the operator on '0'.

Entertainment Information

The *Village Voice* newspaper has a complete listing of all music, theatre, cinema and other entertainments in New York for the coming week. It is published every Wednesday and is available from all newsstands. Friday's *New York Times* contains an informative *Weekend* section with good events listings. The *NewYorker* magazine's *Goings On About Town* section has a weekly events listing, as does *New York Magazine*. The *City Lights* section in Sunday's *News* is good for reviews.

Entry Formalities

Passing through Immigration in New York is a formal, time-consuming and somewhat daunting experience. Before you arrive, on the aeroplane or

Don't harbour any doubts about Manhattan's island status

ship, you will be asked to complete an immigration form. Details required include name, address, flight details, the address of wherever you will be staying, the nature of your visit (whether business, pleasure, etc) plus the date you intend to leave. What the Immigration officials basically want to know is that you can support yourself while on US soil. To apply for a visa extension or a permit to re-enter the US, contact the US Immigration and Naturalization Service, 26 Federal Plaza, NYC (tel: 206 6500).

Guided Tours

Boats

A **Circle Line** Boat Tour offers spectacular proof that Manhattan is an island. Commentators entertain with 'facts, lore and humorous trivia', such as a brief résumé of Yankee Stadium which, when rebuilt, lost hundreds of seats because the new ones needed to be four inches wider to accommodate a much expanded population. The tour cruises past magnificent views of skyscrapers, covering 31 miles (50km) in three hours, and several leave every day from Pier 83 at the far western end of 42nd Street. There are two a day in winter, rising to approximately one every 45 minutes in high summer, but no tours between January and February (tel: 563 3200). Visitors on a tighter budget can get the best view of the skyline and the Statue of Liberty from the **Staten Island Ferry** (tel: 718-390 5253). Other guided cruise companies include **TNT**

Hydrolines 1¼ hour catamaran cruises, departing from Pier 11, foot of Wall Street and East River, Monday to Saturday at 12.00 and 14.00hrs (tel: 244 4770) and **Seaport Line** (90-minute excursions from Pier 16, South Street Seaport, on turn-of-the-century-style vessels; tel: 385 0791 for schedule).

Buses
Gray Line, 900 Eighth Avenue, between 53rd and 54th Streets (tel: 397 2600). These buses have been showing New York to the millions for the last 70 years. There is a choice of over 20 tours, from two hours to all day, covering such areas as Radio City Music Hall, the historic Hudson Valley and, for gamblers, Atlantic City on the New Jersey shores. Other bus tour companies include **Campus Coach Lines** (tel: 682 1050), **Shortline** (tel: 354 5122) and **Academy Bus Tours** (tel: 964 6600).

Driving
Brian Prinsell's five-hour tours

Taking in the rush of the city at a gentle pace from a buggy

take in the other NY boroughs (tel: 718 238 0133). Companies offering limousines for private sightseeing tours include **Manhattan Limousine** (tel: 800 221 7500), **Gordon's Limousine Service** (tel: 921 0081) and **Gotham Limousine** (tel: 868 8860).

Helicopter
Helicopter bird's eye panoramas of the skyline, Central Park, Manhattan's bridges and the Statue of Liberty, by day or night, on a 10-minute hop, daily 09.00-21.00hrs (until 18.00hrs January to March). Details: Island Helicopter, East 34th Street heliport on the East River (tel: 683 4575).

Horse-drawn
Buggy rides: as an alternative to walking around Central Park, take a gentle clop around the perimeter in the back of an open-topped horse-drawn carriage. Tours leave from the southern end of the park.

Walking
Talk a Walk, 30 Waterside Plaza, Apartment 10D (tel: 686 0356). Cassette tapes cover the history, architecture and legends of Manhattan. The recordings come with a map and cover two walks each. **Landmark Tours** (tel: 979 5263) cover everything from 'The Brooklyn Bridge by Twilight' to 'NoHo and The East Village'. The **Museum of the City of New York** (tel: 534 1034) have been organising Sunday tours for six months of the year for 30 years. **Urban Park Rangers** (tel: 360 8194) arrange free

walks and workshops in the parks of all five boroughs. **Greenwich Village Walking Tours** (tel: 675 3213) offer an insight into Village highspots. The **United Nations** (tel: 963 7713) arrange tours of the General Assembly and Secretariat.

Health Regulations

Vaccinations are not required but medical insurance cover of at least $1,000,000 is strongly recommended. If involved in an accident in New York you will be cared for by medical services and charged later.

Holidays

Some of the dates given may vary from year to year.
Public holidays:
1 January: New Year
January (third Monday): Martin Luther King Day
February (third Monday): Washington's Birthday
17 March: St Patrick's Day
March/April: Good Friday
May (last Monday): Memorial Day
4 July: Independence Day
September (first Monday): Labor Day
9 October: Columbus Day
11 November: Veterans' Day
Late November: Thanksgiving
25 December: Christmas Day
Boxing Day is not a public holiday in the US.

Lost Property

If you lose something in a taxi, phone 840 4734. On a train phone Amtrak (tel: 736 4545). On a bus or subway (tel: 330 3322).

Media

Newspapers and Magazines
The broadsheet *New York Times*

Baseball in Central Park – the centre of a city at play

is published daily with a bumper Sunday edition. The two tabloids are the *Daily News* and the more sensationalist *New York Post*, the latter owned by Rupert Murdoch's News International Group. The two most interesting magazines for the visitor are the *New Yorker*, published weekly with cartoons, essays and short stories, and *New York Magazine*, a more yuppie-style, again Murdoch-owned publication. Overseas newspapers and magazines are sold at The Magazine Store, 30 Lincoln Plaza.

TV and Radio

The choice of viewing is very wide. The 30 or so channels fall under two umbrellas, Broadcast and Cable, the latter available to anyone who subscribes.
For quality documentaries, plays and educational programmes tune into Channels 5, 13, 25 and 31, the PBS (Public Broadcasting Service) channels. Popular

programmes are the 24-hour CNN (Cable News Network), the films on HBO (Home Box Office), and the rock and pop videos on MTV (Music Television). Full details are in the weekly *TV Guide*.

The most popular radio stations are on FM:

WNYC: 93.9 – classical music and an excellent morning news programme

WPCJ: 95.5 – endless pop and rock chart hits

WKCR: 98.9 – for jazz

WBAI: 99.5 – general current affairs and features

BBC World Service is on 49m short wave.

Money Matters

Dollar bills come in one, two (rarely seen), five, 10, 20, 50 and 100 denominations. One dollar is made up of 100 cents in coins of one cent (or pennies); five cents (nickel); 10 cents (dime) and 25 cents (a quarter). Local calls from public telephones cost 25 cents; any combination accepted except pennies. Parking meters take

Emporium of the radical chic: SoHo's stores look more like galleries than shops

dimes. An unlimited amount of dollars can be imported or exported, but amounts of over $10,000 must be reported to US Customs, as should similar amounts of gold.

Do not leave home without either American Express, Visa, Access (known as Mastercard in NY) or Diners cards. Always carry US dollar travellers' cheques since they can be used as cash. If you need to cash a travellers' cheque or exchange currency out of hours, try **Chequepoints**, 551 Madison Avenue at 55th Street, (open 07.30-22.30hrs, seven days a week) or **Deak-Perera**, 41 East 42nd Street at Madison Avenue (open Monday to Friday 09.00-17.30hrs, Saturday 17.00hrs).

Opening Times

Shops: most shops open six days a week, and generally open their doors at about 10.00hrs. They stay open until 18.00hrs or later, with one late night (around 21.00hrs). Many shops also open on Sundays, from around noon to 17.00hrs.

Banks are usually open 09.00-15.00hrs or 15.30hrs. A few stay open later on Thursday or Friday.

Pharmacist

There is a pharmacy on almost every block, open from Monday to Saturday 09.00-18.00hrs. The **Duane Reed** chain is a discount equivalent, ideal for basic requirements as well as toiletries and stationery. Drugstores sell medicines for minor ailments. For out-of-hours emergencies **Kaufman**, 557 Lexington Avenue (tel: 755 2266) is open 24 hours.

Places of Worship

There are over 2,500 places of worship in New York, of every religious denomination. The *Yellow Pages* is a good listings source.

The bigger places of worship include Calvary Baptist Church, 123 West 57th Street; St Patrick's Cathedral (Catholic), Fifth Avenue at 50th Street; Presbyterian Church, Fifth Avenue at 55th Street; Temple Emanu-El (Jewish), Fifth Avenue at 65th Street; Holy Trinity (Lutheran), Central Park West at 65th Street; St Thomas' Church (Episcopal), 1 West 53rd Street; and Lexington United Methodist Church, 150 East 62nd Street.

Personal Safety

See **Crime** and **Personal Priorities**.

Police

Police headquarters are in the Civic Center. Dial 911 for emergency or use one of the clearly marked street phones, which have a direct line to emergency services. Each district has a police station; to find your nearest one phone 374 5000.

Post Office

It is notoriously difficult to find anywhere to buy a stamp in New York. The main branch of the US Post Office is on Manhattan's West Side at 421 Eighth Avenue and 33rd Street, NY 10001, open 24 hours (limited service on Sunday). Other branches are scattered throughout the city and blue mail boxes are on street corners. Stamps are sold from machines in shops and supermarkets but you pay a lot more than their face value. Hotel desks can provide many mail services.

Public Transport

New York's mass transport system is extensive, fast and extremely efficient. For full details of all the services call **NYC Transit Authority Information Bureau** (06.00-21.00hrs, tel: (718) 330-1234). Maps are available from the information booth at Grand Central Terminal or the New York Convention and Visitors Bureau (see **Tourist Offices**) or subway token booths.

Bus: though often hot in summer and crowded, buses are obviously more scenic than the subway. Over three dozen services operate, mostly running along the avenues, *ie* north to south, with cross-town services available every 10 or so blocks. Bus stops are close to street corners, every two or three blocks, indicated by red, white and blue poles with route numbers marked. You must enter at the front of the bus and pay a flat fare of $1.25 (no change given): drop your coins or subway token into the fare box next to the driver. If you need to change buses ask the driver for a free transfer ticket.

Bus routes beyond Manhattan and into upstate New York are served by **Greyhound** buses (tel: 635 0800), **Shortline** (tel: 354-5122) and **Hampton Jitney** (tel: 895 9336), who serve Long Island.

DIRECTORY

The colour of transport – the Greyhound bus and the yellow cab

Subway: the days of the noisy, dirty subway are receding. The subway offers the fastest way to travel, and the most frequent service, especially if you use the express trains which rattle through various stations, 'leapfrogging' along the routes. There are five main stop-at-every-station services which run parallel along the length of Manhattan's main avenues. Each subway carriage carries a map of the whole system. Buy tokens at the entrance to the stations and drop one in a turnstile to gain access to the platform. Both subways and several buses operate their services throughout the night, though it is inadvisable to take the subway after midnight.

Taxi: the familiar yellow cabs and their either highly articulate or downright morose drivers are one of the sights and sounds of the city. When available for hire they display an illuminated sign on the roof, and they can be hailed anywhere on the street, though there are a few taxi ranks. Payment is according to the meter, based on a standing charge and a per mile cost,

with night-time surcharges. They are legally bound to take you wherever you want to go within the five boroughs, though you will have to pay any bridge or tunnel tolls, including Newark, JF Kennedy and La Guardia airports. A 20 per cent tip is expected nowadays.

Trains: for passenger timetable enquiries on the national rail company, **Amtrak**, call 800-872 7245. Amtrak serves local stations to the north and south of the city; trains leave from Grand Central Terminal and Pennsylvania Station. The **Long Island Railroad** (tel: 739 4200) serves the north and south shores of Long Island and destinations in Queens from Pennsylvania Station. **PATH** (tel: 466 7649) commuter trains serve Newark, Jersey City and Hoboken in New Jersey from several different stations in the city.

Senior Citizens

Senior citizens will find discounts on many attractions. Men must be over 65, women over 62. You will usually be asked to show your passport.

Student and Youth Travel

Students are entitled to discounts in many attractions. You will need to show proof of your student status, with an International Student Identity Card, and evidence of your age. For YMCA details see **Accommodation**, page 85.

Telephones

'Long distance' means any call beyond the 212 area code of Manhattan and the Bronx.

Brooklyn, Queens and Staten Island are in the 718 area code. Dial 1 plus the area code (when you are outside the area you are trying to reach).

Most phone booths take all coins except pennies: it costs 25 cents for the first three minutes of a local call. When phoning abroad from the US dial 011, then the country code followed by the local code – leaving out the initial zero – and the local number.

Country Codes:
Australia 61
Canada 1
Eire 353
New Zealand 64
UK 44

From a public telephone dial 0 for the operator and then give the name of the country, city and telephone number you are calling: directory enquiries in New York is 143 (you will need at least $5.50 in quarters). For information on international calling, phone the toll-free number 1 800 874 4000.

Time
New York (Eastern Standard Time) is five hours behind Greenwich Mean Time, 14 or 16 hours behind Sydney and 16 or 18 hours behind New Zealand for most of the year. Daylight saving hours are in force between early April and October.

Tipping
Always give cabbies, barmen and waiters at least 15 per cent. Waiters and waitresses, in particular, rely on tips as a major part of their income,

designed to encourage them to give good service. As a general guideline tip 50 cents per bag for a porter at the hotel, and for the doorman who hails you a taxi (more in deluxe hotels). In restaurants the simplest way to work out how much of a tip to give is to double the New York sales tax of 8.25 per cent.

Toilets
The standard of cleanliness in American lavatories, even in the dingiest café, is very high. Ask for the bathroom, or the restroom.

Tourist Offices
The **New York Convention and Visitors Bureau** is at 2, Columbus Circle (where Eighth Avenue, 59th Street and Broadway all meet), New York, NY 10019 (tel: 397 8222); open 09.00-18.00hrs, from 10.00hrs at weekends. Its shelves contain a wealth of brochures, pamphlets and listings on the city. There is another branch based in Times Square at 158-160 West 42nd Street. **New York State Division of Tourism**, 1 Commerce Plaza, Albany, NY 12245 promotes the whole state of New York (written enquiries only). In the UK, contact the US Travel and Tourism Administration, PO Box 1EN, London W1A 1EN (tel: 071 495 4466) (written enquiries only). Australians or New Zealanders should contact: Suite 6106, MLC Centre, King and Castlereagh Streets, Sydney, New South Wales 2000 (tel: 612 233 4666).

INDEX

INDEX/ACKNOWLEDGEMENTS

ACKNOWLEDGEMENTS

The Automobile Association would like to thank the following
photographers and libraries for their assistance in the preparation
of this book:

DOUGLAS CORRANCE took all the photographs not listed below
(AA Photo Library).

NATURE PHOTOGRAPHERS LTD 47 Central Park (D Washington),
48 Blue Jay (J Hancock), 49 Poison ivy (A J Cleave), 52 King crab, 55
Soras Rail (P Sterry).

ZEFA PICTURE LIBRARY UK LTD Cover: Statue of Liberty.

Thanks also to **Mick Sinclair**, and **The Port Authority of New York
and New Jersey** (London) for their assistance in updating this
revised edition.

For this revision: Copy editor and verifier Jenny Fry